THE GOOD FATHER

THE GOOD FATHER

KEYS FOR OVERCOMING IN THE STRUGGLE
FOR IDENTITY, BELONGING, AND BETTER
RELATIONSHIPS

Paul Butler

CrossLink Publishing

CrossLink Publishing
558 E. Castle Pines Pkwy, Ste B4117
Castle Rock, CO 80108
www.crosslinkpublishing.com

Ordering Information:
Quantity sales. Special discounts are available on quantity purchases by corporations, associations, and others. For details, contact the "Special Sales Department" at the address above.

The Good Father/Butler —1st ed.

ISBN 978-1-63357-149-5

Library of Congress Control Number: 2018946196

First edition: 10 9 8 7 6 5 4 3 2 1

This book is dedicated to my parents, Tim and Edith Butler.

I so wanted to place this book in your hands and see the pleasure on both of your faces—but you were called home before I could finish it. So, this dedication will have to do for now. Thank you for your deep love, for your faithfulness and perseverance, for your wonderful example and steady support, and for always being there. And Dad, thanks for that simple prayer you prayed all those years ago that started everything...

Contents

Preface

This book has been twenty-five years in the making, more or less. Not the actual writing of it, but rather the twists and turns of my personal journey that led to the writing. The details of that story could fill another book, but here are the broad strokes.

My wife and I, along with our three boys, were missionaries in Congo (formerly Zaire) for nearly seven years. We loved it. I loved it so much that I never wanted it to end. I had finally found a place where I truly belonged, a ministry at which I excelled, and along with it, an **identity** of which I was proud. My African coworkers even gave me a name to go with that identity: *Mwana Mboka*, which means "village kid," or "native-born." It seemed I had left my feelings of inadequacy—and along with them the habit of always comparing myself to others—back in the States, and well in the past. And then one day, our beautiful life began to crumble as gunfire rang out, the pillaging started, and a mob tried to bash in the doors to our house. My dream-come-true was over.

We soon found ourselves back in America, feeling lost and bereft. I was angry at the unfairness of it all. I had been somebody that mattered, doing something that made a difference, and now I was a nobody again, a complete zero, back to square one. I couldn't see any future that could possibly be better than what I had just lost. I stayed angry for the next year, and stubbornly clung to my hopes of returning to Africa while trying to beat back renewed feelings of failure and inferiority.

Thanks to a congregation who welcomed my family and me in this difficult season, and who made it their business to love us and include us in their lives, my heart began to soften. And then Jesus came to the rescue. A season of revival and refreshing came to our community of believers, and along with many others, I received grace to make a fresh surrender of my life to the Lord. I spent the next eight months or so immersing myself in the gospels and in prayer. I began to see things I had never seen before, and I began to grasp my true identity as a beloved son, rather than as a second-string servant. I learned that I was someone with a place at the family table and an identity that went much deeper than any job description. It's an identity that is not dependent on any human measurement of success or failure. I began to experience, and maybe even to understand in some small measure, the overcoming love God has for us.

All that study and prayer eventually led to sharing in churches, teaching, and counseling more than a few hurting people. It was a huge learning curve, and listening to one story after another, I began to realize how many of us struggle against insecurity, a nagging sense of failure or disappointment, and often a crushing loneliness. It also became evident that we needed more than some inspirational preaching, as encouraging as that can be. We needed a foundation on which to build (or maybe rebuild) our relationships, as well as a template for personal growth. About this time, some friends who worked with YWAM (Youth With A Mission) invited me to teach a course entitled *The Father-Heart of God*, in a discipleship training school in West Africa, and then in the Philippines. I needed to dig deeper if I was really going to help anyone, and most of the material in this book is a result of that search.

The notes I developed were at first nothing more than scribbled outlines with arrows connecting this thing and that, circles around key words, and additional thoughts (which sometimes came to me in the middle of teaching a class) scribbled in the margins. No one else could have made sense of them! I made attempts over the years to better organize these notes, but I had no thought of writing a book. Then, four years ago, I learned that I was in the last stage of a rare and incurable cancer. I thought I was going to die, but many people prayed, and instead of dying I recovered. But that got me thinking... It was time to write, so that these simple principles that had helped a number of people over the years could continue to help many more people for years to come—whether I was able to stick around or not.

It was much easier teaching the truths you will find in this book that it was writing them out in manuscript form. Teaching is a dynamic process, involving interaction with students, room for questions and answers, and the ability to make adjustments or clarifications as you go. Nothing is set in stone. Writing about biblical/spiritual topics is scary, though, because I can't see your face and gauge your reaction to what I have written. Instead I have to carefully consider exactly how to say what I want to say so that it will be clear to you rather than confusing at any point— and this process has taken more than a little time! The actual writing has taken place sometimes at my desk here at home, and other times at a cancer treatment clinic while I sat for hours each week with an IV line in my arm—munching on pretzels and tapping away on my iPad—or during many nights in a little mud-brick house in a rural African village. (The night sounds of an African village make a great backdrop for writing!)

I owe many thanks to my amazing wife, Cindy, who gave me so much helpful feedback during the writing process, along with the encouragement to keep at it. Also I give thanks to Sue Hines, who agreed to read the manuscript with a sharp eye before I submitted it to my publisher, and who offered not only lots of corrections but helpful suggestions, as well. Thanks go to my brother, David, who read it all and assured me that yes, this was important stuff that needed to be published. I also want to acknowledge my friend and coworker Paula Brander, who is part of the backstory of this book. She was my interpreter and fellow minister year after year in West Africa as I shared this message with students, until I was finally able to teach it directly in French. I want to thank the YWAM bases in Mali, where I have had the privilege of developing and sharing the message of The Good Father over the past twenty years. What an adventure and privilege it has been!

To you, the reader, may this book be an agent of transformation and something that will help you along in your journey to the Father.

Paul Butler
April 24, 2018

Introduction

For this reason I kneel before the **Father, from whom every family in heaven and on earth derives its name**. I pray that out of his glorious riches he may strengthen you with power through his Spirit in your inner being, so that Christ may dwell in your hearts through faith. And I pray that you, **being rooted and established in love, may have power, together with all the Lord's holy people**, to grasp how wide and long and high and deep is the love of Christ, and to know this love that surpasses knowledge—that you may be filled to the measure of all the fullness of God (Ephesians 3:14–19, emphasis mine).

Father. There is probably no word that carries with it more emotional impact, more associations, more longing, more expectations or disappointments—and that can elicit a more visceral response—than this one word. For some, it brings instant comfort and a smile; for others, maybe unspeakable pain, or a vague sense of loneliness. There are times when I've introduced that word into the conversation and it has produced an involuntary sneer and a bitter comment: "What a worthless piece of !" In some cases, the word *father* brings nothing more than a memory of standing at a window, watching and waiting for the man who never showed up. And then there are those who would like nothing better than to excise the very concept from their lives, who pretend that in their case, such a thing never existed and doesn't even matter. "You can't miss what you never had," they argue. But they are wrong. Very wrong.

No matter how you relate to the word or the idea of a *father*, it's as impossible to remove the concept from the human psyche or from the realm of human experience as it would be to remove the sun from the sky or the earth from beneath your feet. Our earthly fathers have shaped our lives—whether by their presence or by their absence—in significant and inescapable ways.

In biblical thought, *father* is the original reality, not only behind the visible creation, but He exists as the very source of Family—that intimate network of *relationships* into which we are born, in which we learn what it is to be human, what is our identity, and what it looks like to be connected to others. It is from that small circle of relationships that we are launched out into the much wider world of human society (whether we are ready or not), navigating according to the relational rules we have learned. The apostle Paul describes God as "The Father, from whom every family in heaven and on earth is named." In New Testament Greek, *pater* is "father," and *patria* is "family." The latter cannot exist without the former. Father and family are not merely societal inventions that we have then transposed onto God. Family, and human relationships in general, exist *because* there is a relational being, an original Father, at the back of everything. And He is good to the very core.

Relational Pain

According to the biblical record, human life began in the context of an intimate relationship between God and man. God said, "Let us make man in our image and in our likeness...." We are given a bit more detail in Genesis 2:7: "Then the Lord God formed the man of the dust from the ground and breathed into his nostrils the breath of life, and the man became a living creature." This is entirely different from the way God created all the other living creatures, who came to exist simply because He spoke. He gave the royal command, "Let there be," and the sky was filled with things that fly, the sea with things that swim, and the earth with all manner of beasts "after their kind"—as opposed to "in the image of God." When it comes to the creation of man, the Scripture shows God being involved on a much more intimate level, **forming** the man, as a potter forms something from the clay with his own hands, and then breathing His own life—His own Spirit—into this personal masterpiece. "Into his nostrils," it says. And the man became a living being. When life, intellect, volition, emotion, desire, sensation, all that makes us human, first awoke, and that first man became a sentient being, he was face-to-face with Father God. This is how life began for Adam, within the intimate, close-as-breath gaze of his Creator. He was loved, cherished, and known. It was within that gaze that he knew God, and in the same instant he knew himself. Here is the foundation of human existence, and it's why we can't live without connection, without communication, without loving and being loved, without belonging.

Relationships are as essential to life as air and water, and our souls know this. But this is also where humankind experiences its deepest pains and its greatest struggles. I'm convinced that some of our most painful suffering, and certainly the most pervasive, is that suffering we experience in the realm of relationships. In our attempts to make those life-giving connections, to know and to be known, to belong, to find what we need, and to be what someone else needs, there lies the possibility of wonderful healing or devastating wounds. We live in a world that is disconnected from the Father, a world where so many of us are walking around with gaping holes in our souls; crippled, or at best stunted in our ability to build healthy relationships. We try to cope as best we can, muddling through, knowing it should be better than this, but with no clear idea of what is wrong or how to fix it... But there is good news!

There is a way back to the Father, back to a secure foundation, back to the very source from which your life springs. It's a place where the deep needs you never knew you had will be filled, where your soul can be restored, and where you will learn the meaning of the word home. Once your soul has settled into this place, your story will make sense, your identity will be made clear, and your future will look different from your past. Jesus came into the world to seek you out and to lead you to this place—back to the Father's house.

"I am the way, the truth and the life. No one comes to the Father, except through me" (John 14:6).

Part One: Made for Relationship

1

The Father Foundation

I have a friend who likes antiques. One day she found an antique recipe for a cake—a chocolate cake, I think it was. She was excited to try it, something from a bygone era that she could re-create in her own little kitchen! She carefully mixed together all the ingredients and popped it into the oven, but when she opened the oven door to check on it a while later, there was no cake, antique or otherwise—just a bubbling mass of goo. *What happened?* she said to herself. *I followed the recipe.* What happened was that the most basic ingredient of any cake—flour—had not been listed. I guess this baker from the olden days simply assumed that everyone would know that flour was needed, and that they would add it in the appropriate amount, because you can't have a cake without it! My friend eventually realized what the missing ingredient was, started over, and baked the best chocolate cake ever.

Likewise, there are some basic relational ingredients to a sound, healthy life—things that God the Father provided for His kids at the very beginning, and that every father after Him was meant to provide—but they are often overlooked or left out of our family recipes. Things that should be obvious, at least in an ideal world, are not. We may have the feeling that something important is missing, but we just can't put our fingers on it. When our first parents, Adam and Eve, lost their intimate connection with Father God, they were crippled in their ability to effectively pass on these essentials to their children, and so the cycle has continued for generations. Many of us have grown up with holes in our souls, deficits of which we are only vaguely aware and that, as adults, we unconsciously expect others to fill. In most cases, parents love their children. They do the best they know to do and they give the best they have; our physical needs for food, clothing, shelter, and safety are met. But when it comes to our inner person and the formation of our relational selves—our souls—we will usually get from our parents some version of what they received from theirs, for better or worse. We can only give what we have received.

I want to share with you two biblical principles that are always helpful for personal growth, but especially so when we feel stuck, when we are struggling to move forward in relationship with God and others.

1) Go back to God's original design.

Isaiah 51:1 says: "Listen to me, you who pursue righteousness and who seek the Lord: Look to the rock from which you were cut and to the quarry from which you were hewn."

In this passage, the Lord is telling His people, Israel, to remember their origins as a nation, beginning with Abraham and Sarah and God's faithfulness to them, and to return to the principles embodied in the life of their founding father. For us, we need to go back even further, to the ultimate Rock, the original Father, from whom all life springs and in whose image we were made. And that's what we're going to do in this chapter.

2) Examine your life in light of God's original design.

Lamentations 3:40 says: "Let us examine our ways and test them, and let us return to the Lord."

We're going to take a look at God's original design for relationship with His children, and the things He provided as a secure foundation in that relationship. Then I'm going to challenge you to examine your experience in light of this original "father foundation." One of the functions of God's Word is to expose the holes in our souls, so that we can recognize our need and look to Him for the provision that will heal, strengthen, and enable us to move forward in paths of righteousness, i.e., right relationships with other people.

The Father Foundation

At this point, it would be good to thoughtfully read through the first three chapters of Genesis in order to appreciate God's intentions and plans for His first children, and to understand the context of their interactions. We're going to identity four relational essentials that God provided for Adam and Eve, things that I believe were intended to serve as a solid foundation from which the first human beings could launch out and fulfill their destiny.

1) Presence

Genesis 3:8 states: "Then the man and his wife heard the sound of the Lord God as he was walking in the garden in the cool of the day, and they hid from the Lord God among the trees of the garden."

Although God's presence is not explicitly mentioned until we get to the tragic account of Adam and Eve's rejection of their relationship with God in Genesis 3, God's presence permeates the story from the very first word. Implicit in the narrative is the fact that **He is there**, not only for the work of creating, but once that work is finished, He is still there—guiding, instructing, accompanying, and watching over His children. He doesn't simply set the world in motion and then back away. His overarching presence is the very environment in which they live. This is such a basic fact that it tends to be overlooked. But this is bedrock and more necessary than the earth under our feet. Without it we are in a freefall.

Simply stated, the provision of **presence** answers that basic human need to know that there is someone bigger, stronger, and wiser who is there and who is taking care of things—taking care of me! Presence says, "You are not alone in this world, you're not on your own. It's going to be okay." Presence says, "The weight of the world is not on your shoulders." **The provision of presence is the root of security**. Without it we grow up anxious, tense, fearful, and nearly always in fight-or-flight mode. Without presence, you can never let down your guard, never trust, never rest—and this is an unbearable way to live.

It is no coincidence that repeatedly throughout the Old and New Testaments, God says to His people, "Don't be afraid, I am with you," or "I will be with you." Presence—to not be left alone—may be the deepest need we have, and abandonment may be our greatest fear. From the time when Adam and Eve broke their intimate connection with God and were banished from the Garden, that fear of being cut off, abandoned, and left alone took root in the human heart. This explains, at least in part, so many of our desperate attempts at connection, no matter what it may cost us.

2) Affirmation, or Words of Blessing

Genesis 1:26–28 reads: "

> Then God said, 'Let us make mankind in our image, in
> our likeness, so that they may rule over the fish in the
> sea and the birds in the sky, over the livestock and all
> the wild animals, and over all the creatures that move
> along the ground.' So God created mankind in his own
> image, in the image of God he created them; male and
> female he created them. **God blessed them and said
> to them**, 'Be fruitful and increase in number; fill the
> earth and subdue it. Rule over the fish in the sea and
> the birds in the sky and over every living creature that
> moves on the ground' (emphasis mine).

From the outset, our first parents received **words of blessing**
that were intended to empower, inform, and direct them into
their destiny. Adam and Eve heard and received these powerful
words of blessing and affirmation *at the very beginning* of their
adventure, and this is how they were launched into their life and
their mission. They began with the Father's words of approval
and affirmation ringing in their ears: "This is who you are, and it
is good! This is what you can achieve because I have empowered
you. Now, go for it!"

They did not step into life tentatively, full of self-doubt and insecurity, wondering, *Can we do it? What if we fail? What if we're not
good enough, or strong enough or smart enough?* Their Father God
had already answered all of these questions before they even had
a chance to ask. Adam and Eve knew who they were, they knew
their destiny, and they knew that it was all good as they looked
to and listened to their Creator. Many years later, Moses said to
the nation of Israel, "Man shall not live by bread alone, but by
every word that proceeds out of the mouth of God." Centuries
after Moses, Jesus took His stand on this truth at the outset of His

earthly ministry. In the beginning, this is how our first parents lived. Their understanding of themselves, of God, of the world around them, and of how they fit into it was totally dependent on what God said to them. To put it another way, they lived by divine revelation rather than by human reasoning.

Every human being born into this world comes into it with these questions: "Who am I? Am I worthy? Do you like me? Do you want me?" For better or worse, the first answers we receive to these questions come from our parents or adult caregivers. We are entirely dependent on the "big people" to explain the world to us, and little children naturally believe what the big people say. If you're a parent—or even if you've simply held an infant— you've noticed the fascination that little baby has with your face. Infants, and then toddlers, are looking there for answers to those questions. I believe that more than trying to know you, that child is looking into your face to know himself and his place, to know what you think of him. What is reflected in the parent's face, and later what is communicated through a parent's words, will determine how the child sees and understands himself. To make a generalization, for boys the question is usually "Am I strong? Am I capable?" And for girls, it often takes the form "Am I beautiful? Do you like me/want me?"

How often has a little boy attempted some feat of strength— picking up what is to him a heavy object or climbing the lower branches of a tree—all the while shouting to his father or mother, "Look at me! Look what I can do!" He's looking for the thumbs-up sign, anxious for those words of approval: "Wow! You're the man, look at how strong you are!"

How often has the little girl twirled around in a new outfit, or done a cartwheel, shouting the same: "Daddy, look! Look at me!" She's fully expecting to hear, "Wow! Don't you look beautiful!"

or "Wow! You're amazing!" When we did these things as children, it was not simply to get attention; it was to get an answer to that burning question.

How that question was answered over time as we grew up and developed a sense of identity—or whether it was answered at all—has a powerful impact on how we see ourselves and how well-adjusted we are in this world. There are countless adults still searching, sometimes in all the wrong places, for the answer. But this is something God the Father provides for all His kids: words of blessing and affirmation. We'll talk more in a later chapter about hearing the Father's voice and receiving the words He has for each of us.

3) Intervention/Active Involvement

One thing we see about God in these first three chapters of Genesis is that He is not passive or distant when it comes to His children. It was noted in the introduction that the very manner in which God created mankind was unique, as opposed to how the universe and even the other living creatures were brought into being. The heavens and the earth were simply spoken into being as the Almighty issued a series of royal commands. It was the same for the flora and the fauna in their various forms—each was created and designed to produce "after its kind." Such is the power of God's creative word. But when it came to the creation of man, man was not created "after his kind" (suggesting a certain limitation—a cow can only ever be a cow and nothing more), but in the "**image of God**." Something of God's very nature and person was invested in man, which suggests a deep, personal connection between him and his Creator. To go a step further, we notice that God did not speak mankind into being, but instead "formed the man from the dust of the ground and breathed into his nostrils the breath of life." This reveals a degree of personal, intimate involvement beyond anything we see with the other elements of creation.

After this, Adam is not simply left in the garden to figure things out for himself. Father God is there, giving direction, explaining the boundaries, and interacting with Adam in his work. He is given enough space to exercise his God-given authority and abilities, but also enough space to experience need—a deep need for human companionship that he cannot fill for himself. And again, God is active, intervening to create woman, equally made in His image, and to present her to the man as his counterpart and partner.

Although it is not explicitly stated in the text, we get the idea that God would come into the Garden regularly to walk and talk with Adam and Eve. They are given freedom and the opportunity to work, to discover, and to choose, but they are never left alone! Even when the worst happens—when they disobey and rebel, choosing independence from Father God in place of the intimate relationship they had known—God is not passive or distant.

> But the Lord God called to the man, "Where are you?" He answered, "I heard you in the garden, and I was afraid because I was naked; so I hid." And he said, "Who told you that you were naked? Have you eaten from the tree that I commanded you not to eat from?" (Genesis 3:9–11).

Here is the original Father, seeking out His first children when they have strayed, calling out to them, confronting them, giving them an opportunity to confess and return. And when their disappointing response is to point fingers and cast blame, He calls them to account. With words that I am sure made their lips tremble and the tears flow, He brings the discipline that will save them from a fate worse than death. Yes, they are banished from the Garden, but they are never ignored or left alone. The true Father is never passive or distant when it comes to His children, but always actively involved, because those made in His image matter to Him.

Such involvement from parents—and especially on the part of fathers—is a basic need that every child has. Involvement and action communicates value to a child, just as passivity on the part of a parent says, "What happens to you, what you do, and who you become really don't matter to me. You are not that important." In the long run, this is crippling. As a Father, God is active and involved, whether for direction or for discipline, comfort, or instruction. Learning to embrace that, however, can be difficult—especially if you're used to being left on your own.

4) Belonging

> And now, Father, glorify me in your presence with the glory I had with you before the world began (John 17:5).

Somewhere in my journey as a follower of Jesus, I heard a ridiculous idea expressed—an attempt to answer the question, "Why did God create man?" It was suggested that somehow God was tired of being all by Himself in heaven, so He created man in order to have someone with whom to fellowship! While it is true that we were created in order to be in relationship and partnership with God, the need and the privilege is ours. The glory is His. He has never been lonely! He has never needed us for anything. He is the only Being in the universe who is absolutely self-sufficient, and the idea that God created man out of some sense of lack, some need that He had, is a blasphemy. A god who is needy and hungry, who feeds off of his creation—this is an entirely pagan idea that has nothing to do with the God who is revealed in Scripture.

In eternity past, before there ever was a world, the divine community of Father, Son, and Holy Spirit existed—a dynamic family circle of overflowing glory, joy, love, power, and fullness. Jesus touched on this in His prayer in John 17, as He anticipated returning to the Father. The apostle Paul describes God the Father as the One "who fills everything in every way" (Ephesians 1:23). The entire creation is an expression, an overflow of this fullness. Man was created out of this fullness, this overflow of love, to participate in this fellowship, and to be **included** in this original family circle. **We were made for belonging.**

On the relational level, Adam and Eve came into being within this family circle—with all the dignity of free, volitional beings, but at the same time belonging to the divine family. This belonging was not something to be earned; they were "born' into it." This is why repentance and faith are so often pictured in Scripture as "coming back" to God, or coming home—because this is where life began for humanity, this is our true home, and this is what we have lost through sin and rebellion. On the physical level, Adam and Eve also belonged in a unique way to the earth, being formed from it, and God the Father prepared a physical place of belonging for them—a home—in the Garden. Just as there was an accord between God and man, there was also an accord between man and the earth that he had been commissioned to care for and develop. It was a place where they were completely at home.

Loss of belonging was one of the great tragedies of man's rebellion against God, one of the most grievous results of rejecting the relationship with the Father that is the foundation of everything. It's no surprise that loneliness, "lostness"—that feeling of never quite fitting in or truly belonging, of always being on the outside, has nagged the human race ever since. Nothing stings quite like being left out! We're desperate to belong. The good news of the Gospel is that Jesus, the true Son of the Father, came to bring us back into the family circle, and He has prepared a place of belonging for us.

In the next chapter, we're going to talk a bit more about what life looks like when any of these four foundational elements has been lacking during our formative years. We'll examine the deficits—the holes in our souls—and how these deficits have shaped our thinking, our behavior, and maybe even how we relate to others. But we're certainly not going to stay there! Our only purpose for looking at the past is to better understand ourselves in the present, allowing God to straighten what is bent and to fill the empty places so that we can confidently move into the future He has planned for us.

2

Confronting Our Brokenness and Finding Wholeness

Before we take a closer look at the possible holes in our souls, the lack in our relational foundations, and how that lack might affect our lives and relationships even into the present, we need to take a good look at God's original, glorious intention for humanity. The gospel is God's restoration program, not simply an insurance policy against the fires of hell. Colossians 3:10 describes a "new self, which is being renewed in knowledge in the image of its creator." As we follow Jesus and seek to know the Father better, we are being re-created, renewed, and restored—but restored to what, exactly?

Romans 3:23 is a well-known and often-quoted verse about our need for rescue and restoration. It says: "For all have sinned and fall short of the glory of God."

I think that most of us understand clearly enough the "all have sinned" part, and we can easily call to mind specific sins we've committed. But what about the "fall short of the glory of God" part? When we talk about the *glory of God*, we don't want to cheapen it by imagining that this verse is simply referring to a set of rules that we have failed to obey. The glory of God is infinitely grander than that! It is the glory of God's person, His character, His image—and we were made for **that**, to share in the divine nature, to reflect the image of God, and to carry it into this world. **You were made for glory**. There is an original, glorious you that God has always had in mind, and He wants to bring you back to that.

If you've spent much time in the Bible-believing world, you may be wondering about this idea. You may be thinking, *Hold on a minute. Doesn't the Bible say that God will not share His glory with anyone?* To answer that question directly, no. The Bible does not say that. Through the prophet Isaiah, God says very clearly that He will not share the glory for His great deeds with idols or with false gods. (See Isaiah 48:3–11.) But human beings, on the other hand, were **made** for the glory of God. There was an original glory that the Father intended for us, but we missed it; we "fell short" of it when we sinned and decided to go our own way. In His great mercy, God initiated a recovery plan in Jesus. Here is what Jesus Himself said in John 17:8, as He prayed for His disciples:

"The glory that You have given me I have given to them...."

Wow! We'll talk more about this later, but for the moment, suffice it to say that God's original intention for us was about *much more* than simply managing to keep all the rules. Hebrews 2:10 states that God's plan is to "bring many sons to glory" through the ministry of Jesus. Each of us is unique and has been created to reveal God's glory in a way that no one else can, but rather than leave you with a vague idea of what it means to be restored to that original glory, I'd like to give you some *specific aspects* of God's glory in mankind. These are specific elements of our Father God's original intention for us. Many of us live with an almost constant, vague sense of frustration and failure—that somehow we are not doing enough, or not doing it well enough, or not being good enough. And this frequently results in us comparing ourselves to others in an effort to find some practical standard of measure, or simply to assure ourselves that we're no worse than the next guy. But we know deep down that this is a futile exercise.

The most practical—and life-giving—thing we can do is to lift up our eyes and take a good look at the original glory with which man was crowned. These are things for which you have been made:

- **Dignity, not disgrace.** This is the most basic aspect of God's glory in man. Dignity derives from the fact that we were made in the image and likeness of God, and therefore we are capable of a level and a quality of relationship with Him—a familial relationship—that neither animals nor the angels can experience. This is borne out in the New Testament, where we read that Jesus, the Son, came to bring many sons to glory and is "not ashamed to call them brothers."

- **Authority, not slavery.** In Genesis 1:26 we hear God saying, "Let us make man in our image, in our likeness, **and let them rule....**" God did not create mankind because He lacked servants. He wasn't looking for a labor force. There were already myriad angels who exist to carry out His orders. His plan was to have *sons and daughters* who would understand His intentions, bear His authority, and live in partnership with Him to carry out His will on earth as it is done in heaven. It was the authority to do good. They were divinely empowered to cultivate and develop—not pollute or destroy—the earth.

- **Productivity, not futility.** "And God blessed them and said to them, 'Be fruitful and multiply, fill the earth...'" (Gen. 1:28). I believe this original blessing of fruitfulness extends beyond the simple ability to conceive and bear children. It includes the creative power to harness the resources of the earth, the potential of opportunities, and the abilities of our own bodies and minds, to be fruitful and productive in our work and to bring blessing to the world.

- **Intimacy, not loneliness.** This aspect of God's intention for our first parents may not be explicitly stated, but it is certainly clear as we read the first three chapters of Genesis. From the tender details of the Father's creation of Adam in chapter 2, to the open communication they enjoyed in the garden; from God's declaration (after having declared everything good) that it was "not good" for the man to be alone, to the creation of woman and the final, profound detail at the end of this account that "the man and his wife were both naked and were not ashamed," it is clear that intimacy was a vital aspect of this original glory for which we were made.

God never abandoned His original design—these things still stand as His will for each one of us. But since these aspects of glory flow from the Father's very nature, *it is no use trying to reclaim them by simply adjusting our thinking and trying harder.* What we need is to be rooted and grounded in the Father's love, as the apostle Paul says in Ephesians 3:17, to be established on that foundation where our most basic needs are met and the holes in our souls are filled and—just as importantly—where we learn the truth.

We've already noted that after Adam and Eve broke their relationship with the Father God, they were impaired in their ability to adequately provide to their own children what they had received, those basic things that every father is meant to provide. In our broken world, there is dysfunctional parenting, there is adequate parenting, and there is even some very good parenting, but no earthly parent is perfect. Now it's time to examine those empty places in our own souls and to recognize the ways that we've attempted to compensate, so that we can turn with honesty to the perfect Father who meets every need.

Learning, Beliefs, and Behavior

It would be a mistake to underestimate the importance of our formative years. From infancy through adolescence, we are avid learners and keen observers, our minds and hearts processing enormous amounts of information—most of it taught not in a classroom, but in the context of family and primary relationships. We are learning from the adults and from everyday experiences who we are, how we fit in the world, what is our worth, what is important in life, how to get what we want or need, how to make friends and navigate social situations, and sometimes how best to simply survive. We are developing our "practical theology"—a set of beliefs and assumptions that will largely dictate our behavior as we move into adulthood—usually without even realizing it!

To pretend that all of the influences, the experiences, and the beliefs we developed during those years have no bearing on our adult lives would be foolish. It would also be foolish if we never examined them in the light of God's Word or allowed our assumptions to be challenged. This is so important because there is an enemy of souls who seeks in every way possible to drive a wedge between us and Father God. The devil is not nice, and he doesn't play fair. If he can use the imperfections and failures of our parents—or of any adults whom we loved and trusted as children—to lie to us about ourselves, the world, or even God

Himself, he will do it. He's been doing it ever since Genesis 3! Thankfully, we have the Scriptures. Hebrews 4:12 says:

> For the word of God is alive and active. Sharper than any double-edged sword, it penetrates even to dividing soul and spirit, joints and marrow; it judges the thoughts and attitudes of the heart.

It is the function of God's Word to expose and confront the false beliefs that are usually deep-rooted in our hearts. When we come to Christ and choose to entrust our lives to Him, we accept the Word of God—a new set of beliefs that we hopefully begin to explore and act upon, and through which we will be gradually transformed. But a host of basic, often unconsciously held beliefs, which we developed as we grew up, are still operating under the surface and driving much of our thinking and behavior. We can go through life with these two layers of belief:

1. The Word of God, which we accepted when we chose to follow Jesus. We may be truly sincere in our acceptance of and desire to follow this new way, but there is usually another deeper layer of beliefs that we developed over a lifetime...
2. The "thoughts and attitudes of the heart" that often drive our behavior.

It is usually when we are in stressful or crisis-fraught situations, when we feel threatened, that those underlying beliefs will surface and dictate how we react. My prayer is that in the remainder of this chapter, you will find the Word of God gently exposing and confronting false beliefs and fears, and speaking into the empty places that your heavenly Father wants to fill. So, let's explore together...

Filling in the "Blanks"

Most of us have taken those "fill in the blank" exams during our school years. These were more difficult than "multiple choice" exams, in which several possible answers were provided and you just had to pick the right one. With multiple choice exams, even if you hadn't studied, you could make an educated guess, because the correct answer was right there in front of you somewhere on the page. But with a "fill in the blank" test, if you hadn't studied or payed careful attention in class...well, there was that sinking feeling as you made a wild guess, or just sat there paralyzed.

When any of the basic elements of the "father foundation" that we've already listed—presence, blessing, intervention, and belonging—are missing, we are left on our own to fill in the blanks with something—anything—in order to survive and move forward in life. The answers we come up with on our own are usually not the best, and they are often at the root of our relational difficulties. Let's take a look at 1 John 2:15–16:

> Do not love the world or anything in the world. If anyone loves the world, love for the Father is not in them. For everything in the world—the lust of the flesh, the lust of the eyes, and the pride of life—comes not from the Father but from the world.

When the Scriptures speak of "the world" in this context, it is not talking about people as individuals. God loves people and wants everyone to return to Him. But here, the Bible is talking about the world system—society as a whole—which lives independently from God as its Creator and Father, that lives by its own strength, by its own wisdom, and that rejects any idea of dependence on or submission to a higher power. When we are not experiencing the love of the Father, who knows exactly how to fill those blank spaces, we will inevitably be influenced by the world.

In other words, the desires of the flesh (our felt needs, both physical and emotional) will dictate our thinking and behavior. The "desire of the eyes" (a focus on the false images of wealth, success, beauty, and power that the world presents to us) will enslave us. The "pride of life" will require that we build up and present a false front of strength and invincibility to others. Life becomes a never-ending cycle of trying to get something and trying to prove something. This uphill climb often leads to a meltdown of exhaustion, depression, severe anxiety, and mental paralysis. Eventually, we manage to get ourselves up off the floor and start the whole thing over again, hoping it will be different this time. You are not alone! Maybe you will recognize a little bit of yourself as we look in further detail at those blank spaces...

The Absence of Presence

One of the sweetest aspects of childhood is trust: that simple knowledge that someone bigger, stronger, and wiser than me is **there**. He is taking care of things, taking care of me, and I don't have to worry. He is available if I have questions, if I am afraid, if I need help or comfort. He loves me. I am safe. The steady **presence** of a father provides security, builds confidence, enables trust, and lays the foundation for future trust in a heavenly Father as we are launched into adulthood. But what happens when presence is absent? If you've grown up with the absence of a father or a father figure—or maybe with one who was "there, but not really *there*," not available or engaged—how might that have shaped you? Here are some common traits of someone who has missed presence in his or her life:

- The belief that "I am on my own in this world. I can't depend on anyone but myself." You tend to feel responsible for everything and everyone; the world is on your shoulders. This often results in a hardworking, hard-driving lifestyle and a likelihood for outward success, but your relationships may suffer because there is little left over for you to invest. "If you want something done right, you have to do it yourself" is your motto.
- High stress and frequent bouts of anxiety, maybe even panic attacks. You always feel under pressure. It's hard work running the world, but somebody has to do it!
- A deep sense of loneliness and isolation. Difficulty connecting with people beyond surface communication. As a believer, difficulty experiencing or feeling the presence of God. He seems distant.
- Depression and exhaustion when the load becomes too much.
- Distrust of authority, resistance to even healthy authority, and a tendency to withdraw and do your own thing versus being part of a team.

The Absence of Blessing and Affirmation

As children, we are always looking to parents or other important adults for the "thumbs-up" sign; we have a natural desire to please. We need to know that we're okay and that we're doing well, that we're capable of success. To clarify here, I am not talking about rewards without effort or special prizes just for breathing. Blessing and affirmation says, "I like you! I believe in you! You have great worth and potential. You can do it!" Blessing and affirmation builds into children a strong sense of identity.

In far too many families, words of blessing and affirmation are few and far between. Parents are often tired, stressed out, and impatient, with the result that words of criticism and frustration are readily expressed. Instead of blessing, cursing is the result. More than once, I've witnessed a harried mother herding a toddler from the parking lot into a store with the words, "Come ON! Hurry UP! Do you think I have all day!?" All of it shouted in an annoyed, angry tone of voice. Or when the drink spills at the fast-food restaurant: "What's wrong with you!! Look at this mess!"

These messages—yes, when you're a child, you just got a clear message—*distort reality*. The truth is, a toddler isn't capable of walking as fast her parent. It's a physical fact. But the child is shamed and rebuked for something she can't change, for simply being a child. Message received? "There is something wrong with you. You're slow, and you're not capable since you should be able to keep up. You're making life hard for Mom." When the drink is accidentally knocked over, the reality is that accidents happen. Small children are clumsy because their fine motor skills are not yet fully developed. But when Jimmy is publicly berated and shamed for an accident, the message that is being hammered in is that he is stupid, inferior, and a nuisance. And Jimmy doesn't have enough knowledge or experience to reject that lie.

Unfortunately, that's far from the worst I've heard as I've counseled and prayed with people struggling to believe they are worth anything at all... Messages like this are all too common:

"You're worthless! You'll never amount to anything!"

"You're lazy just like your no-good father!"

"You're treacherous just like your mother!"

"You're so stupid! It's a shame you couldn't be more like your sister—she's the brains of the family."

What are the results of all of this?

- You experience inferiority, that conviction that you are less intelligent, less capable, less worthy than the average person walking around on the planet. You believe you'll never be as capable as others. The biblical word for this is *shame*. You feel guilty for everything—even for breathing air and taking up space—and you want to apologize for your very existence. (I may be exaggerating a bit here, but not *that* much for some of you.)
- You are timid and lack confidence in work or social situations. You do your best not to be noticed and to stay out of the way. "I'll never fit in anywhere" is what you believe.
- A strong façade of competence and respectability is the flipside of this. Appearance management is vital, because what people think is all-important!
- Comparing yourself to others is a way of life.
- You are unable to receive criticism, even when the intent is constructive. It feels unbearable, and you either become fiercely defensive or totally dejected. ("Why even try? I'm a failure anyway.") At the same time, you are uncomfortable with praise or compliments, and so you deflect them. No one is allowed to contradict your negative opinion of yourself. It's oddly comforting to affirm your misfit status.
- You are secretly ashamed of how much you crave approval as an adult. It is truly an addiction. (Social media was *made* for this!) You need to be frequently convinced that you're not a loser.
- You have a weak or nonexistent sense of personal identity. You tend to constantly adapt yourself to be what you think others want you to be to win their approval.
- Follow-through on long-term goals is difficult for you. Because you're always a failure, it doesn't matter anyway.

The Absence of Intervention and Active Involvement

Just as being involved and playing an active role in a child's life communicates value and worth, passivity and disinterest on the part of a child's parents communicates the opposite: "You don't matter all that much; you are not that important." We've seen in the first three chapters of Genesis that God the Father took an active role in the lives of His children, communicating, explaining and teaching, intervening, and even disciplining them—all because *they mattered* to Him. And you matter to Him, as well. He cares about the direction of your life and what happens to you.

In my time as a pastor and missionary, I have counseled more than a few individuals who were sexually abused as children, often by a relative or close friend of the family. In nearly every case where this confused, frightened young person found the courage to say something to a parent, he or she was told in no uncertain terms to "never talk about such things again!" or, "Don't make a fuss about it; these things happen." Sometimes the abuse stopped, in some cases it continued, but it was never directly addressed. The message to the child in each instance was clear: *You don't matter that much, and it's okay if bad things happen to you. No one will defend you.*

Being defended, or having a parent stick up for you, is not the only form of intervention we need as children. A father's active role in enforcing boundaries and providing discipline or training is also critical to a child's development.

Dan and his wife came to see me. Their marriage was struggling due to his passivity and lack of confidence. Having grown up as an only child in a very quiet, lonely household, in which interaction between Dan and his parents was always at a minimum, Dan got into some serious trouble with the law during his teenage years. He got drunk and stole a car. He told me with a stricken, disbelieving look on his face that his father never said *anything* to him about the incident. Nothing. His dad was completely passive. His parents did accompany him to court, where he was given probation. Then they went home, and the incident was never spoken of again. Dan craved something, anything, from his father—some reaction, some punishment, a lecture at least! Anything but the passive silence, as if he was invisible in the household. And so he punished himself—believing that no one else was going to do it—by not leaving the house all that summer.

When parental involvement has been largely absent during our formative years, we may enter adulthood with the following issues:

- Lack of purpose and direction
- Difficulty making and maintaining commitments
- Passivity when we know some action or decision is needed. Difficulty in making decisions and following through, or feeling "paralyzed"
- Lack of confidence to initiate or lead, whether in work or social situations
- Feelings of worthlessness and futility (that *What's-the-use?* feeling)

Loss of Belonging

In healthy families, children are given a strong sense of belonging—the understanding that they are part of something good and important. They are included rather than ignored. That means being included in household chores that contribute to the family's well-being, as well as times of family fun and times of celebration. Belonging is every child's birthright. If I experience rejection at school or on the playground, it's not the end of the world, because the people who really matter to me love me, and I have a place of belonging with them.

Unfortunately, in poorly functioning families, parents are often harried and overwhelmed with the basics of survival and providing the bare necessities. There seems to be little energy left over for including children in household activities, for creating that "our family" place of belonging, for holding that son or daughter close for some "snuggle time," or for reading a book together. Children are then left with a feeling of being in the way, rather than wanted and included. It can create a lonely world, that is made worse by the inevitable rejection encountered at school when they didn't make the team, didn't get invited to the party, or didn't get to sit with the popular kids at lunch.

And then there are the truly heartbreaking cases (and I've known more than a few) where a child has been clearly told in word and deed that he is not wanted and is actually in the way...

Whatever the situation, it's easy for rejection to become the dominating theme that we experience as we move into adulthood. Here are some common issues when a child grows up with a rejection mentality:

- Being hypersensitive to any possibility of rejection and easily offended. You may feel that you are being deliberately left out of things, even when that's not the case.
- Always waiting to be included, or specifically invited, to activities or events that are open to everyone, and feeling slighted if someone doesn't beg you to join in.
- Feeling easily threatened by people you see as more popular, more capable, or better at something than you are—and you will jealously protect your position.

- Swinging between periods of almost total withdrawal from social situations, to an almost frantic attempt to be included in everything.
- Sometimes fulfilling your expectation of being rejected, by being contrary, difficult, or even obnoxious, and thus rejecting others *before* they can reject you. Or swinging to the other extreme, which is...
- Experiencing an extreme fear of abandonment and willingness to do almost anything in order to not be alone, including tolerating abuse and unhealthy situations.

All of the above are common manifestations of brokenness—things that may point to the holes in our souls that God wants to fill as our loving, all-sufficient Father. I'm not a doctor of psychology or of psychiatry, and the above lists are not meant to be used to diagnose any mental health issues. Rather, these are common themes that have surfaced time and again in my twenty years of teaching the Bible and conducting pastoral counseling, because they are common to the human race. I have also become convinced through these years of experience that our good, good Father is able to heal every wound, fill every empty place, and straighten every crooked way in our souls as we see Him more clearly through the Scriptures, and as we choose to entrust ourselves more fully to His care.

3

Hearing the Father's Voice

And a voice from heaven said, "This is my Son, whom I love; with him I am well pleased" (Matthew 3:17).

Jesus answered, "It is written: 'Man shall not live on bread alone, but on every word that comes from the mouth of God'" (Matthew 4:4).

"In the past God spoke to our ancestors through the prophets at many times and in various ways, but in these last days he has spoken to us by his Son, whom he appointed heir of all things, and through whom also he made the universe" (Hebrews 1:1–2).

In our less-than-perfect world, communication is a necessity that is full of pitfalls and that takes lots of work to get right. Opportunities for misunderstandings abound, even when everyone is speaking the same language. When you're communicating cross-culturally in a second or even a third language, the chances of getting it wrong increase exponentially! As I've been learning to function and teach in French over the past several years, I've made my share of mistakes in both speaking and listening. Sometimes I've totally misunderstood what I've heard, which is both frustrating and sometimes really embarrassing! I have a missionary friend who, in his first attempt at preaching in French, repeatedly said the opposite of what he was intending to say. Without giving you a lesson in French pronunciation, I'll just say that there's a tiny difference between saying, "The heroes of faith" and "The zeroes of faith"! Over and over again, while he thought he was encouraging people with stories of the heroes of faith, he was enthusiastically referring to them all as the **zeroes of faith!** Oops. The audience had a good laugh, but of course, they understood what he meant to say.

When it comes to understanding God and His attitude toward us, He has always spoken clearly enough, but early on in the story, something went wrong with our ability to hear.

We understand from Scripture that the universe was formed by the word of God, and we see in the first chapters of Genesis that from the start of human history, God the Father was speaking in order to give shape and meaning to the lives of His children. We could safely say that human life began within the sphere of the Father's voice. In the first chapter of Genesis we find those initial words of blessing with which Adam and Eve began their lives— words that gave identity, purpose, and direction. (See Genesis 1:28.) In the next chapter, God continues communicating, defining existence, setting boundaries, and giving instruction. In the beginning, our first parents "lived by every word that comes from the mouth of God" (and not by a list of rules from a book). They lived by divine revelation, which was imparted in the context of an intimate, loving relationship with their heavenly Father. Whatever they knew, whatever they understood about themselves, about God, and about their world, they knew *because God Himself explained it to them.* To be sure, there must have been plenty of discovery for Adam and Eve in this brand-new world, but it was all within the context of the knowledge of God, within the realm of the Father's voice.

Revelation Receivers and Meaning Makers (or Interpreters)

Human beings are designed by God to be *revelation receivers*. What I mean by this is that we were not created with complete knowledge and understanding of all things. We were created with the ability to learn, to discover, and to grow in knowledge and understanding, but God the Father never intended that we should attempt to figure out life on our own, independently from Him and apart from divine revelation. God created us to be dependent on Him and to be taught by Him about who He is, who we are, and what our life is all about. In the Bible, this context of revelation is called the "knowledge of God." Of course, there is something in us that rebels against such dependence—it rubs against our pride, and we'd rather write our own stories and make up our own definitions—but without the knowledge of God, we are running blind and so often living on false assumptions. To understand how we ended up like this, there is another fact of life of which we need to be made aware.

We are not only revelation receivers, but we are also "meaning makers," or *interpreters*. We want to know why, and we are constantly looking for the meaning behind things. It is almost like a reflex for us to interpret others' words and actions, tone of voice, and facial expressions, to discern what they "really mean." What was the intention behind the words or actions? (Have you noticed what a difficult thing communication can be?) When it comes to the larger realm of life events and circumstances, we do this almost unconsciously and on a daily basis. We interpret what is happening (and, of course, we usually see ourselves at the center, with things happening *to* us and events going either *for* or *against us*), and we make assumptions about God, ourselves, others, and life in general.

Now, what is the basis for our interpretation? We interpret based on what we believe and based on the voices we listen to—this world is full of voices vying for our attention and offering to interpret our personal stories for us. And that brings us to the saddest chapter in the Bible.

Another Voice

"It's all good." This has become a common phrase we use these days to smooth things over when something is actually *not* good, when something is, in fact, bad, but we're just going to smile and make the best of it. In the opening chapters of Genesis, however, it really was *all good!* We read five times in the creation account in Genesis 1 that "God saw that it was good." And then the sixth time, "It was very good!" This was God's own assessment of creation, His interpretation of the situation into which He would place His children. As we move on in the story, we see that God caused to grow in the garden "every tree that was pleasing to the sight and *good* for food." The only thing that wasn't good was for the man to be alone, and God in His goodness had a beautiful plan all ready to remedy that problem before Adam even recognized it existed. Can you pick up on the not-so-subtle theme here? God is good, His plans are good, and His intentions toward mankind are all good! So, how did it all turn so bad?

When we arrive at Genesis 3, we can see that another voice—a smooth, seductive, wise-sounding voice—begins to speak. This voice offers another, twisted interpretation of Adam and Eve's life, circumstances, and relationship with God:

Now the serpent was more crafty than any of the wild animals the Lord God had made. He said to the woman, "Did God really say, 'You must not eat from any tree in the garden'?" The woman said to the serpent, "We may eat fruit from the trees in the garden, but God did say, 'You must not eat fruit from the tree that is in the middle of the garden, and you must not touch it, or you will die.'" "You will not certainly die," the serpent said to the woman. "For God knows that when you eat from it your eyes will be opened, and you will be like God, knowing good and evil" (Gen. 3:1–5).

With just a few cleverly crafted phrases, Satan (taking the form of a serpent) accomplished several things in his quest to destroy the intimate relationship between God and His children.

- He suggests that God is being unreasonable and unfair. ("You're really not allowed to eat from all these beautiful trees? That's harsh!")
- Instead of being good, he suggests that God's intentions are actually sinister and that His goal is to keep Adam and Eve ignorant and under His thumb.
- At the same time, he suggests that Adam and Eve are inferior in their current state of innocence, with the words, "You will be like God, knowing..."
- To sum it up simply, Satan was saying, "God is not really good, and you're not really good enough! But just listen to me, because I'm here to help..."

Our first parents *were already as much like God as they needed to be*, having been made in His very image! They were already more like God—having something of His very nature in them—than any angel or spirit being could ever be!

Let's reflect for a moment on what is happening in this scene. Up until this point in the story, has anything actually changed in Adam and Eve's circumstances? God is still the same, good to the very core, just as He has always been. The garden is still there, with every kind of tree that was a delight to the eye and good for food—including the Tree of Life—and they had access to all of this! Every need they had was filled, along with a healthy dose of pleasure and delight. These first human beings were still living in the glory of God and bearing the image of God in a garden paradise. We know what happens next. But why? Why did Adam and Eve take the forbidden fruit and choose to reject their relationship with the Father in favor of independence from Him?

The answer is that **one thing**—and only one thing—had changed. Their **interpretation** of their circumstances and their view of life had changed radically as they listened to the serpent's suggestions. Suddenly, at least in their minds, God was not as good as they had thought that He was. He was depriving them of something they needed, so how could they still trust Him? They themselves were no longer good enough. Now they felt inferior and foolish. All that God had provided was not enough anymore—they couldn't even see it. All they could see was the one thing that they **couldn't** have, and that life could never be good unless they had it. They needed to take matters into their own hands... immediately.

This same scenario has been played out in people's lives down through the ages, and it continues to this day. **No matter the specific circumstances, or how cleverly it's presented to us, at the root of all of our false beliefs and crazy behaviors is the age-old lie that God is not good, and that we can never be good enough.** This lie has skewed our interpretation of life over and over, like a faulty roadmap that lands us in a ditch every time.

It was because our first parents accepted this twisted interpretation of their circumstances that they made that fateful choice to break their intimate relationship with the Father—and the loss has been incalculable. Among other things, they lost their ability to truly hear the Father's voice and to interpret life correctly. They "lost" those original words of blessing that God had given them at the start (see Gen. 1:28)—or maybe we could say that they removed themselves from the influence of those life-giving words. Let's have a look at Genesis 3:8–10:

> Then the man and his wife heard the sound of the Lord God as he was walking in the garden in the cool of the day, and they hid from the Lord God among the trees of the garden. But the Lord God called to the man, "Where are you?" He answered, "I heard you in the garden, and I was afraid because I was naked; so I hid.

Do you see it? The same Voice—that wonderful voice of the Father that used to bring joy, comfort, and reassurance—now struck terror in their hearts. God was actually calling out to them in mercy because He wanted to give them an opportunity to reconcile, but instead of mercy, what they heard was the menacing, threatening voice of punishment. And people have been misunderstanding God ever since. Jesus said to the Jews, who felt threatened because He would not operate according to their rulebook:

> "Why do you not understand what I am saying? It is because you cannot hear My word. You are of your father the devil, and you want to do the desires of your father. He was a murderer from the beginning, and does not stand in the truth because there is no truth in him. Whenever he speaks a lie, he speaks from his own nature, for he is a liar and the father of lies.

But because I speak the truth, you do not believe Me"
(John 8:43–45).

When we have been listening to other voices and living outside
the realm of the Father's voice, truth can be difficult to listen to
and receive. Our instinct for self-protection kicks in, and truth
starts to feel threatening because it often challenges our status
quo. When all the lies we have listened to feel so familiar, we will
put up walls against the truth.

When Adam and Eve could no longer hide, they resorted to
blame—doing anything but dealing face-to-face with the One
who had been their intimate Father and Friend. Since that time,
the human race has been estranged from their original Father
and living out of range of His voice. But God never has stopped
speaking and working to win us back.

God Is Still Speaking, but Now It's Up Close and Personal

Let's take a look at Hebrews 1:1–2:

> In the past God spoke to our ancestors through the
> prophets at many times and in various ways, but in
> these last days he has spoken to us by his Son, whom
> he appointed heir of all things, and through whom also
> he made the universe.

We have seen how our first parents rejected an intimate, face-
to-face relationship with God the Father, and as a result, they
shrank back from His voice. With a few notable exceptions, this
became the pattern for mankind. But God continued speaking
and reaching out through His intermediaries—through prophets and teachers, through acts of mercy and amazing rescues—at
many times and in various ways. One of the most memorable of

THE GOOD FATHER • 47

those ways is found in Exodus 20, where the Lord makes a covenant with the nation of Israel after rescuing them from Egypt. Here was the people's response to God's voice in this situation:

> When the people saw the thunder and lightning and heard the trumpet and saw the mountain in smoke, they trembled with fear. They stayed at a distance and said to Moses, "**Speak to us yourself and we will listen. But do not have God speak to us or we will die.**"
>
> Moses said to the people, "Do not be afraid. God has come to test you, so that the fear of God will be with you to keep you from sinning."
>
> **The people remained at a distance**, while Moses approached the thick darkness where God was" (Exodus 20:18–20, emphasis mine).

They still didn't want a direct, face-to-face encounter with the Lord. Instead, they said: *Moses, you can go and listen to the Lord for us and tell us what He says. We'll trust you to deal with God on our behalf. We'll obey everything He says, but we'd rather not have any more direct encounters with Him, okay? Way too scary!* And that's pretty much the way things continued throughout the Old Testament period. But it wasn't going to stay that way!

The Lord never gave up on His original plan to have sons and daughters who would walk in intimate relationship and open communication with Him. This has always been God's intention. Let's now take a look at Hebrews 8:7–12:

> For if there had been nothing wrong with that first covenant, no place would have been sought for another. But God found fault with the people and said:

"The days are coming, declares the Lord, when I will make a new covenant with the people of Israel and with the people of Judah. It will not be like the covenant I made with their ancestors when I took them by the hand to lead them out of Egypt, because they did not remain faithful to my covenant, and I turned away from them, declares the Lord. This is the covenant I will establish with the people of Israel after that time, declares the Lord. I will put my laws in their minds and write them on their hearts. I will be their God, and they will be my people. **No longer will they teach their neighbor, or say to one another, 'Know the Lord,' because they will all know me, from the least of them to the greatest.** For I will forgive their wickedness and will remember their sins no more."

To me, this is the most precious promise in the entire Bible—the promise of a new kind of relationship with God, based not on a rulebook but on personal, direct, face-to-face communication with the God who forgives my sins and writes His love and mercy on my heart. To bring this about, prophets and go-betweens would never be enough. When the time was right, God began speaking to everyone with ears to hear, in the most personal, self-revealing way possible—through His Son. If you want to know what God is saying, listen to Jesus and look at Jesus. That's why His words and His deeds are so faithfully recorded in the gospels of Matthew, Mark, Luke, and John.

Hebrews 1 goes on to say that Jesus is "the radiance of God's glory and the exact representation of His being." Nothing secondhand here—and no chance of misinterpreting what God is saying!

The Voice from Heaven

> As soon as Jesus was baptized, he went up out of the water. At that moment heaven was opened, and he saw the Spirit of God descending like a dove and alighting on him. And a voice from heaven said, "This is my Son, whom I love; with him I am well pleased (Matthew 3:16–17).

What we see here is the inauguration of Jesus' public ministry. In the Bible, beginnings are almost always important—whether it is the beginning of a family, a nation, or a ministry. How something begins usually highlights something important about the character of that ministry and how it will continue. Jesus' ministry began under an open heaven, with the descent of the Holy Spirit, and **under the sound of the Father's voice** announcing words of blessing and approbation.

Why did Jesus need to begin His ministry in this way? He already knew who He was and what was His mission, and He was not insecure nor lacking in direction. So, what was happening here? By submitting to baptism (remember that people were coming to John the Baptist to be baptized as a sign of repentance for sin), Jesus was identifying Himself with sinful mankind—with Adam. **And by His simple, public act of obedience, He received back from the Father those original words of blessing that Adam had lost through his disobedience.** Heaven opened, and God's voice was heard again! Jesus did not need to receive these words for Himself. No, He stood in that place to make room for you, so that you could stand with Him under that open heaven, so that you could hear that same voice and receive those same words of blessing as a beloved son or daughter of God! And Jesus remained within that realm—under an open heaven, empowered by the Holy Spirit, and hearing the Father's voice—throughout His ministry. You can live there, too.

The Challenge and the Choice

The words of blessing that Jesus received from the Father did not go unchallenged—just as those original words of blessing given to Adam were also challenged and contradicted. The familiar story is recorded in Matthew 4:

> Then Jesus was led by the Spirit into the wilderness to be tempted by the devil. After fasting forty days and forty nights, he was hungry. The tempter came to him and said, "If you are the Son of God, tell these stones to become bread." Jesus answered, "It is written: 'Man shall not live on bread alone, but on every word that comes from the mouth of God'" (Matthew 4:1–4).

Jesus was in a vulnerable place, hungry and seemingly alone in a desert. The evil one challenged His identity as the beloved Son, dared Him to prove something, and counseled Him to take matters into His own hands—to act independently from the Father. It seems logical, even reasonable: You're hungry, You have supernatural power, so use it and get what You need in this moment. Jesus chose instead to live "by every word that comes from the mouth of God," rather than to be led by internal needs or external pressures. And that is the gist of the famous Scripture He quoted from Deuteronomy 8:3, which is all about learning to trust and being dependent on God—to truly listen to Him rather than living by our own human reasoning, which so often causes us to misinterpret our circumstances. **Because we were created to live by listening to the Father, our life truly depends on learning to hear His voice.**

By His obedience, by His choice to live by every word of God, Jesus was undoing and reversing Adam's disobedience. He was making a way for us to come out of the wilderness of isolation and estrangement where we live in false assumptions, and return to a life-giving relationship with the Father. Jesus came out of the wilderness in forty days. Ancient Israel refused to listen to God's voice, and as a result they wandered in the wilderness for forty years! The Lord had rescued the entire nation out of slavery in Egypt and led them through the desert to the brink of the Promised Land. They had God's personal promise that He would bring them in, give them victory, and make them fruitful. But when they arrived, they chose instead to listen to another interpretation of their circumstances. Here is the scenario as Moses described it:

> Then, as the Lord our God commanded us, we set out from Horeb and went toward the hill country of the Amorites through all that vast and dreadful wilderness that you have seen, and so we reached Kadesh Barnea. Then I said to you, "You have reached the hill country of the Amorites, which the Lord our God is giving us. See, the Lord your God has given you the land. Go up and take possession of it as the Lord, the God of your ancestors, told you. Do not be afraid; do not be discouraged" (Deut. 1:19–21).

> But you were unwilling to go up; you rebelled against the command of the Lord your God. You grumbled in your tents and said, "The Lord hates us; so he brought us out of Egypt to deliver us into the hands of the Amorites to destroy us. Where can we go? Our brothers have made our hearts melt in fear. They say, 'The people are stronger and taller than we are; the cities are large, with walls up to the sky. We even saw the

Anakites there.'" Then I said to you, "Do not be terrified; do not be afraid of them. The Lord your God, who
is going before you, will fight for you, as he did for you
in Egypt, before your very eyes, and in the wilderness.
There you saw how the Lord your God carried you, as
a father carries his son, all the way you went until you
reached this place. In spite of this, you did not trust in
the Lord your God..." (Deut. 1:26–32).

Do you see how clearly these two competing interpretations are
contrasted? "The Lord hates us, so He brought us out of Egypt...
to destroy us." "The Lord your God carried you, as a father carries his son, all the way you went..." Two entirely opposite interpretations of the exact same series of events, contrasted here in
the Scriptures for our benefit!

It is always our choice either to listen to the Father's voice and
what He says about our life and circumstances, or to accept
some other interpretation that slanders God's character and be-
littles our worth to Him. It seems easy to condemn the ancient
Israelites, who had seen so many miracles, who had so many
proofs of God's love and faithfulness, but who still rejected His
voice. But, in reality, we who are alive today have something
even better than they had back in that time. We have the Father's
voice, made that much clearer in Jesus, who forever remains the
greatest, most solid proof of God's love for mankind and the pure
goodness of His character.

"I Have Given Them the Words..."

To wrap up this chapter, I want to encourage you to believe that
those original words of blessing that God spoke over our first parents, and those words that Jesus received from the Father at His
baptism—the Father's voice as He speaks to us by His Son—are

for you! In John 17, as Jesus was about to complete His mission on earth and return to the Father, He prayed for His disciples. He stated explicitly in this prayer that it was not only for them, "but for all who will believe in Me through their words" (John17:20). That means **you**. As He prayed, Jesus said to the Father:

> "I have revealed you to those whom you gave me out of the world. They were yours; you gave them to me and they have obeyed your word. Now they know that everything you have given me comes from you. **For I gave them the words you gave me** and they accepted them. They knew with certainty that I came from you, and they believed that you sent me" (John 17:6–8).

I believe that Jesus is referring to some very specific words here, not simply the entire body of teaching that He imparted over those three and a half years of ministry with His disciples. Throughout the Old Testament, we can see that it was customary for a father or another leader to impart specific words of blessing to his children or followers before he died and left this world. The words that Jesus received at His baptism, those words of blessing and affirmation, He has now passed on to us, so that we may also live from this place of hearing the Father's voice. Listen to what Jesus said as He continued this prayer for His followers:

> "**I have given them the glory that you gave me**, that they may be one as we are one— I in them and you in me—so that they may be brought to complete unity. Then the world will know that you sent me **and have loved them even as you have loved me**" (John 17:22–23).

Wow! I hope that clears up any doubt lingering in your mind. All the other voices, whether they come from your parents, your peers, your past failures, or your present challenges, will still be there to press their interpretation of life into your ears. But you have a choice to listen to the Voice that came before, and that will still be there after all the others have died away. And that Voice will keep you grounded in the reality of the Father's love.

But What If I'm Bad?

This is a legitimate question. Does God never say anything but soft, comforting, affirming, positive words? Is it all hearts and roses as He speaks into our lives? We'll talk more about how our good Father disciplines His sons and daughters in later chapters, but I want to briefly share a guiding principle here as we close this chapter. Psalm 30:5 says:

> For his anger lasts only a moment, but his favor lasts a
> lifetime; weeping may stay for the night, but rejoicing
> comes in the morning.

Sometimes we've heard a familiar verse so often that we become deaf to what God is saying to us through those well-worn words. So, read it again, out loud maybe. Discipline is a reality, to be sure. But did you get this? In the total scheme of life, discipline only "lasts for a moment." God's favor, however—His kind disposition toward us that wants to bless us and do good in our lives—lasts a lifetime!

Here it is: The everyday environment in God's household is favor; it's love and kindness. That's the general atmosphere in which we are meant to live. His anger, or His discipline, is occasionally necessary, but *we were never meant to live under a continual cloud of disapproval and anger.* God is not a perpetual grouch! But some of us have grown up in situations where anger, irritation, and disapproval dominated the atmosphere—this was the everyday norm—and the experience of actually hitting the mark and receiving a smile of approval was rare. But that is upside-down! When you think about God speaking to you, what do you expect to hear? In these latter days, God is speaking to us through His Son. It's time to start listening to Him and living under His favor.

4

Believing in the Father's Love

> "For my thoughts are not your thoughts, neither are
> your ways my ways," declares the Lord. "For as the
> heavens are higher than the earth, so are my ways
> higher than your ways, and my thoughts than your
> thoughts" (Isaiah 55:8–9).

Have you ever wondered how God feels about you, what He thinks of you, what His attitude is toward you and me? It would be pointless—and presumptuous—to even discuss these questions if we didn't have God's full and faithful revelation of Himself in Jesus. But the fact is, we do have this revelation given to us in the gospels. Hebrews 1:3 tells us that Jesus is the "exact representation of God's being" or nature, and Jesus Himself said that He only did what He saw the Father doing, and that He only said what He heard from the Father. In the book of Revelation He is called "the faithful and true Witness." Jesus never, ever misrepresented the Father; He never exaggerated the truth and He never downplayed it. He faithfully demonstrated it in word and deed. So, if you really want to know what is in God's heart and mind toward you, all you need to do is take a good look at Jesus. Observe His works and listen to His words as recorded for us in Scripture. In this chapter, we're going to look at some of Jesus' interactions with individuals, as well as some of His teachings, and discuss what God is speaking to us through those highlights. Before we do that, however, I want to stress just how vitally important these "snapshots" of Jesus truly are.

As the apostle John closed his gospel account, he wrote:

> Now there are also many other things that Jesus did. Were every one of them to be written, I suppose that the world itself could not contain the books that would be written (John 21:25 ESV).

Think about that for a minute. The gospel writers had some serious editing to do, guided, of course, by the Holy Spirit! There was no way that even *half* of what Jesus said and did could be recorded and included in the accounts of Matthew, Mark, Luke, and John. So, what does that say about the material that *did* make the cut? You can be sure that this material is the "essential Jesus." What we have in the four gospels are the things that most accurately, most powerfully sum up and communicate the Person, the message, and the mission of Jesus—the things that characterize Him best, and the things that indelibly marked His disciples and other eyewitnesses. I am not overstepping my bounds to say that God wants you to take these things—the things He has revealed about Himself in Jesus—seriously. Here is the "gospel truth"...

He Values You Greatly.

> "Therefore I tell you, do not worry about your life, what you will eat or drink; or about your body, what you will wear. Is not life more than food, and the body more than clothes? Look at the birds of the air; they do not sow or reap or store away in barns, and yet your

heavenly Father feeds them. Are you not much more
valuable than they?" (Matthew 6:25–26).

"Are not five sparrows sold for two pennies? Yet not
one of them is forgotten by God. Indeed, the very hairs
of your head are all numbered. Don't be afraid; you are
worth more than many sparrows." (Luke 12:6–7).

In these passages, Jesus was addressing marginalized people who
were living under an occupying army in a politically and eco-
nomically unstable time, seemingly at the mercy of forces beyond their control. These were not the "movers and shakers"
of society; these were the nobodies. And Jesus was saying to
them—and to us: "**The Father wants you to know that your life
matters, that what happens to you matters, that you are not
forgotten by God. He cares about you personally, and He values you greatly!**"

In Luke 15, Jesus told three stories, back to back, about a lost
sheep, a lost coin, and finally a lost son, to underscore the inesti-
mable worth of each individual to God the Father, and His deep
joy when the lost one is found and the wandering one comes
home. This was in response to the religious leaders' assumption
that "sinners" and others who have not kept all the rules were
not worth Jesus' time and attention, if He was really representing God as He claimed. The fact is, your life matters to God the
Father more than you can imagine, wherever you happen to be
on your journey and whether you consider yourself lost, found,
or somewhere in between.

He Knows You Intimately.

This is not a threat—it's a comfort! The Father knows and understands you completely—your great potential, your fatal flaws,

your beautiful gifts and strengths, as well as your hidden weaknesses. In Mark 2:1–12, this scene is portrayed in which four friends were bringing their paralyzed buddy to Jesus. They went to great lengths to bypass the crowd and get their friend right in front of Him. Jesus looked at this man and said, "Take heart, son, your sins are forgiven." There is something going on here that we don't know about, and this young man's friends probably didn't know about it, either, but Jesus looked right into him and knew everything about him. He understood all about the guilt, the hidden shame, and the anxiety this person was suffering through. He knew all of that, and He also knew that the young man knew what He was talking about without any other words being said. Jesus didn't reject him, and He didn't rebuke him. He didn't expose the young man's dirty laundry for everyone to see. (Remember, they were surrounded by a dense crowd.) He called him "son," told him to take heart—or we would say "cheer up!"— shattered the crippling guilt with forgiveness, and then sent him home—healed. That was how Jesus represented the Father, who knows you just that intimately.

Another story that comes to mind is recorded for us in John 4:1– 30, as Jesus passed through Samaria, paused at a well, and had a conversation with a woman whom most people probably didn't talk to. The encounter turned out to be life-changing for her and many others, as well. Jesus knew all about this woman, the fact that she had already had five husbands and that the man with whom she currently lived was not her husband. But from the outset, he treated her with dignity, respect, and kindness rather than with contempt. It was a private conversation, and when Jesus finally brought up her marital status, it was not to condemn her, but to save her. Sometimes the quickest way to the heart is through a wound, and rather than withdrawing in shame this woman responded to the Lord's intimate knowledge of her with faith. Like this woman came to understand, the fact that we are known so fully is an encouragement to draw near in faith, rather than to shrink back in shame.

He Welcomes You As You Are (and He Likes You!)

One of the consistent criticisms leveled at Jesus by the religious establishment was that He was a "friend of sinners," that He spent an inordinate amount of time with people who had issues. And it seemed to the onlookers that He actually liked it!

> Now the tax collectors and sinners were all gathering around to hear Jesus. But the Pharisees and the teachers of the law muttered, "This man welcomes sinners and eats with them" (Luke 15:1).

This was not just a rare crossing over to the wrong side of the tracks to dispense a little mercy, the way some religious groups in our day approach "homeless ministry" or "prison ministry," but it was a regular practice for Jesus. And in that day and culture, sitting down to eat with people meant a level of fellowship reserved for friends. It signaled acceptance and relationship. Jesus was not simply tolerating these people; He genuinely liked being with them, He cared about them, and He accepted them. In that culture, table fellowship meant, "I want you in My inner circle. I want your company."

I know this makes some people nervous, people who will immediately feel the need to remind us all that yes, "although the Father might accept us as we are, He doesn't intend to leave us that way!" As though talking too much about Jesus' acceptance of sinners will give the impression that He condones sin, so we need to constantly remind everyone that He doesn't condone sin, that sinners are expected to change, and that they should hurry up and be quick about it... But if we rush through this part, we're going to miss something really important.

Remember that when Jesus ate with sinners, He was representing the Father. So, what does the Father want us to understand here? I think at least part of it is this: Jesus' focus was not on the *sin*; it was on the *individual* who was made in the image of God. And those are two different things. Jesus was not fellowshipping with sin; He was not interacting and laughing and eating and having conversations with sin, but He was fellowshipping with *people—people* who were designed by God the Father for a good purpose, people who were full of potential, with unique personalities and talents and ways of expressing themselves. Jesus saw and sincerely loved each individual for who he or she was. And yes, He came to save us from the sin that, if left unchecked, would destroy our glorious humanity and personhood.

So, let's talk about you. You are not your sin, and your sin is not you. Sin is not the truest, most basic thing about you. It's an enemy, a destroyer of the real you. The truest, most fundamental thing about you is that you have been uniquely made in the image of God. And God thinks the real you is pretty wonderful; He likes you an awful lot!

Are You Wearing a Burqa?

Before we move on, I want to say one more thing about being accepted by God. In my years since becoming a follower of Jesus (it's been more than forty!), I've heard some teachings about how God the Father accepts us and sees us "in Christ," which is either totally wrong or has been very poorly explained. The idea goes like this: Once you've trusted in Jesus for the forgiveness of your sins and your acceptance with God, from then on, when God looks at you, He doesn't see you anymore. He only sees His beloved Son, Jesus, since you are now "in Christ." Aside from the fact that the Bible doesn't actually say that, what's wrong with this idea?

I recently had a phone conversation with my oldest son, who attended a good Christian school from the time we moved back from Africa to America when he was twelve, until he graduated from high school. He heard this doctrine of acceptance with God (by being in Christ) expounded upon quite a lot, and it came up in our conversation. Here's what he understood as a teenager from the explanations he had heard:

> You are so disgusting and distasteful to God (because of your sin—and you and your sin are basically the same thing) that God can't stand to even look at you. Thankfully, once you believe in Jesus, you're hidden in Christ, and when God looks your way, He doesn't have to see you anymore. He only sees Jesus, and that's how He accepts (or manages to tolerate) you.

How does a teenager—or anyone, for that matter—who is struggling to find his identity, and being encouraged to develop his unique gifts and talents "for the Lord" on the one hand, make sense of something like this on the other? How does one reconcile the encouragement to "Smile, God loves you!" with the idea that "God really can't stand the sight of you"? Does He value anything about my uniqueness (which He supposedly created), and does He even like me—or does He just throw a giant "Jesus sheet" over my head, like a Christian burqa, so that He doesn't have to really look at me? How about you? Are you walking around under a Christian burqa, convinced that God and others wouldn't like the real you?

To be sure, God *never* accepts sin—not yours, not mine, not anyone's—which is why Jesus came to save us from our sins. He didn't come to throw a giant tarp over the whole mess so that God never has to look at you again; He didn't come to obliterate your personhood. To trust in Jesus and to be "in Christ" means that your sins have been forgiven, taken away, canceled, and that **you** have been rescued and brought into the inner circle, where the Father sees you, welcomes you, and delights in you! The apostle Paul describes Jesus' ministry as the ministry of reconciliation and says that "God was in Christ, reconciling the world to himself, **not counting men's sins against them**" (2 Corinthians 5:19). The Father sees you, He likes you, and He's calling you to the table. You can take off the burqa now...

He Loves You to the Uttermost.

Here is one of those well-known passages of Scripture, the scene in which Jesus, about to be betrayed and crucified, washed the feet of His disciples, in which far more is going on than what we see on the surface. Let's take a good look at this passage together.

> It was just before the Passover Festival. Jesus knew that the hour had come for him to leave this world and go to the Father. Having loved his own who were in the world, he loved them to the end.
> The evening meal was in progress, and the devil had already prompted Judas, the son of Simon Iscariot, to betray Jesus. Jesus knew that the Father had put all things under his power, and that he had come from God and was returning to God; so he got up from the meal, took off his outer clothing, and wrapped a towel around his waist. After that, he poured water into a basin and began to wash his disciples' feet, drying them with the towel that was wrapped around him.

He came to Simon Peter, who said to him, "Lord, are
you going to wash my feet?"
Jesus replied, "You do not realize now what I am doing,
but later you will understand."
"No," said Peter, "you shall never wash my feet."
Jesus answered, "Unless I wash you, you have no part
with me."
"Then, Lord," Simon Peter replied, "not just my feet
but my hands and my head as well!"
Jesus answered, "Those who have had a bath need only
to wash their feet; their whole body is clean. And you
are clean, though not every one of you." For he knew
who was going to betray him, and that was why he said
not every one was clean (John 13:1–11).

Most often, this scene is taken as a nice object lesson that Jesus
gave to His disciples about the virtues of humility and service,
and I wouldn't disagree with that point. But before it's about
that, it's actually about something else. Before we start moral-
izing about what we need to do for Jesus and others, we need to
see what Jesus was doing for His disciples here—and what He
wants to do for us.

Think about it for a moment. What are the circumstances sur-
rounding this scene? *When* is it happening? This is literally the
last thing Jesus did for His disciples before His betrayal, arrest,
trial, and crucifixion. This was not just a day like any other day;
something personal, intimate, and powerful was happening here.
John (who, of course, was there) introduced this scene by telling
us explicitly what it was about:

"Having loved his own who were in the world, he loved them to
the end."

The phrase "to the end" here is not simply referring to time, but to the scope and degree of His love for them. It could be translated as "completely" or "to the uttermost." One translation says, "He now showed them the full extent of his love," which I think captures what was really going on here. It's about love. Jesus did something shocking to communicate to His disciples how fully, thoroughly, and deeply they were loved. And remember, in everything He that He did, Jesus was representing the Father.

But washing feet? What did this have to do with love, and why did it have to be **feet**, of all things? It seems kind of unpleasant for the foot-washer, and kind of awkward for the person whose feet are being washed—especially when the one person you respect more than anyone else in the world is the One doing the washing! Just take a few moments to imagine you are there, that you are one of those disciples...

The meal has been a solemn affair. You know something deadly serious is about to happen, and Jesus has clearly said that this is the last meal you're all going to have together like this. The bread is His body, broken. The cup, His blood poured out to make a new covenant... No one knows exactly what to expect, except you know that He's going away—Jesus, the One whom you've grown to love and revere like no other, the One whom you've come to believe is the Messiah, the Son of God, the King who will one day sit on a glorious throne. It's gotten very quiet in the room.

Jesus gets up, takes off His robe, fills a basin with water, and wraps a servant's towel around His waist. This can't really be happening... He's kneeling down in front of John, then James. Time is standing still. Please, someone make Him stop... No, no, no! But everyone is frozen in place, too embarrassed, too ashamed to even move, and the shocked silence deepens, except for the soft scuffling of sandals being removed and pushed to the side, and the water splashing in the basin. Until it's Peter's turn— Peter, who is never afraid to speak up, even in the most delicate of situations. Peter is not going to let this happen. He knows his place, and he knows the Lord's place, and somebody has got to do something to stop all of this!

"Lord, are You going to wash my feet!?"

"I know you don't understand it right now, Peter, but eventually you will."

"Never! Never will You wash my feet!"

"If I don't wash your feet, Peter, then you can't walk with Me."

Then Peter, still trying to control the situation, and probably to deflect the embarrassment he feels (like some of us who can't seem to stop talking when things get awkward), said, "Okay, Lord, then not just my feet, but my head and my hands, too, I'm with You!" But Jesus insisted on just the feet. It's as if He was saying, "You're already Mine, but before you can do something for Me, before you can truly walk with Me in service, **you have to let Me do something for you**, something that will enable you to walk with Me and to follow Me to the end."

Feet are very significant in Scripture, and they speak often of our walk or journey through life, our ability to progress from one point to another, to overcome obstacles and surmount difficulties, and to stand in a position of integrity and victory. In the Bible, we see feet that slip, feet that run to do evil, feet that turn from evil, feet that carry good news or walk on high places, feet that are lame, feet that tread down the enemy and crush serpents, and so on. The first mention of "feet" in the Scriptures comes in Genesis 3:15, where God promised that a descendant of Adam and Eve will ultimately defeat sin and Satan. God said to the serpent, "He will crush your head, but you will bruise his heel." Jesus did defeat Satan by His obedience unto death, and that victory continues to be played out in the lives of those who follow Him to this day.

But in the course of the journey, sometimes our feet get dirty, sometimes they get bruised and wounded, and sometimes we find ourselves moving through life with a limp. Or we're trying our best to hide the dirt or deformity we don't know how to get rid of, and that we are hoping no one will notice. In this broken world, we all walk through stuff, and no one gets out unscathed. But Jesus loves us to the uttermost. He loved each of the disciples enough—even Peter, who would deny Him, and Judas, who would betray Him —to take their dirty, calloused feet into His hands and gently wash them. Without words, He was saying, **"There is nothing about you so unpleasant, no dirt or deformity, no wound or scar, no hidden shame, that would ever cause Me to turn away from you or to stop loving you."**

I believe that Jesus was seeing more than just dirty feet. He was seeing feet that would carry His message into all the world, feet that, though they may have faltered and though they might falter again in the future, would ultimately follow Him to the end. And what about you? If He came to you now—the resurrected, glorified Jesus who has all authority in heaven and on earth—and if He knelt down in front of you to wash your feet, would you let Him? Or would you be in a hurry to kneel down yourself to prove your own devotion to Him? He says, "You have to let Me wash you." Ultimately, the gospel is not about the great things we're going to do for God—it's about the great thing He has already done for us in Jesus. It's about love.

He loves you to the uttermost, and His love is big enough to embrace you in the face of the most unpleasant thing about you. Deep enough to deal with the dirt, gentle enough to heal the wounds, and strong enough to set you on a straight path into life.

> The God of peace will soon crush Satan under your feet. The grace of our Lord Jesus be with you. (Romans 16:20).

Part Two: Breaking Barriers to Friendship with the Father

I n Part One, we've seen God's original design for a close, intimate relationship with us as His sons and daughters, the relational foundation He provides, and how His character and love have been faithfully and powerfully *re-presented* to the world in Jesus. I hope that your mind has become convinced of these truths, and that your heart is saying, "Yes, I want this!" Great! Because now we're going to confront some common relational patterns and behaviors that so often become barriers to our deeper friendship with Father God.

From God's side, there are no barriers. The way is open, and this is precisely what Jesus came to do: to open heaven, to blaze a trail for us back to the Father. Since His death, resurrection, and ascension, heaven stands open and the invitation to come remains as fresh today as it was back then. But so often on our side there is something that seems to block the way, or things that at least make us tentative and cautious in our approach to the Father. Some of those barriers are attitudes and behaviors common to man in our fallen, imperfect world—things we've learned or developed over time in order to cope with life as we've known it. But these things won't help you in your quest for a deeper relationship with God, or with anyone else for that matter!

Dismantling these barriers, unlearning these behaviors, is normally a process—not a onetime, cathartic event. But that's okay, because the process itself is a partnership with the Father, an opportunity to know Him better and to experience more of His transforming grace. One of the things I really love to hear is an unvarnished story of someone in the Bible, someone just like us, whose journey and honest dealings with God have been record- ed for our benefit. We're going to look at a few of these people, and as we're doing that, you might even recognize yourself in some part of their story!

5

Independence versus Intimacy

One thing that began to dawn on me through years of pastoral counseling, sitting in my office with a box of tissues on the desk between me and someone unraveling their story (and people went through the tissues, believe me!), is that there are usually logical reasons as to why people are the way they are. Everyone has a backstory. Realizing this helps us to have grace and patience for others on their not-so-good days—or even for ourselves!

The trick in life is not to allow those reasons to become *excuses*. Excuses mean that we don't really want to change or move forward. Examining our reasons, on the other hand, is a quest to understand the path we've traveled and how we've ended up where we are, so that we can then move forward with more clarity and make better choices for the future. I'm convinced that our Father's love is patient enough and persistent enough to get us moving in the right direction.

Moses was a fiercely independent man who acted rashly and did some pretty drastic things, all on his own, in an attempt to stop the injustices he was witnessing. In his own way, he was only trying to help. It didn't turn out so well, however, and his next reaction was to decide that if people didn't need him, then fine! He didn't need them, either. And so he deliberately distanced himself from nearly everyone for the next forty years. That's a pretty stubborn streak of independence, if you ask me! And the trouble with independence is that it precludes intimacy. Yet at the end of Moses' life, the Bible testifies that he experienced a more intimate relationship with God than just about any other Old Testament character.

> The Lord would speak to Moses face to face, as one speaks to a friend" (Exodus 33:11).

> Since then, no prophet has risen in Israel like Moses, whom the Lord knew face to face (Deuteronomy 34:10).

How does that happen? That's what we're going to find out, but first let's talk a bit about the roots of independence and the tug-of-war we so often experience between independence and intimacy...

The Roots of Independence

We've looked at that first temptation, and at Adam and Eve's fateful decision to disobey God, from various angles. The apostle Paul gives us yet another perspective on that disastrous event. It was a real eye-opener for me.

> For Adam was formed first, then Eve. And Adam was not the one deceived; it was the woman who was deceived and became a sinner (1 Timothy 2:13–14).

At first glance, this sounds like a somewhat unfair criticism of Eve. But if you think about it for a minute, the implications point to Adam's greater responsibility in the whole affair. Paul was say-ing plainly enough that **Adam was not deceived**—but he still ate the forbidden fruit, didn't he? Apparently, with full knowledge of the warnings and consequences, he deliberately, willfully made that move to establish his independence from God the Father. He boldly declared his intention to be his own god rather than to remain dependent on the only true, only good God. And from that moment, there took root in mankind an inner resistance to authority, a rejection of our status as creatures who must always be dependent on their Creator.

From the time we are very young, there is something in us that rises up whenever our parent, or some other authority figure who is there to care for and protect us, draws a line in the sand and says, "No further. Do not cross this line." Immediately, we feel almost compelled to cross that line, to prove that we are in charge of our own lives, that we are not dependent on this other being. That is the root of independence—this desire to be our own gods, to need no one else and to be dependent on no one. But the reality is that we were created for relationship, to need God, to need one another. We were not created to be self-suffi-cient in the absolute sense. Absolute independence is a divine attribute meant for God alone, and an impossible lie for man.

I was an extremely strong-willed child and thought that I should have the right to run my own life as I saw fit, from as early as I can recall. I remember one time when I was about five years old, declaring my firm intention to run away. My mother didn't argue or panic. She packed a nice lunch for me in a brown paper bag, told me to take care of myself and that she would miss me, and sent me on my way. I didn't get very far before I decided to eat my lunch, a little way down the street from our house. I hadn't planned much else beyond that, and sitting there alone was get-ting kind of boring, so I reluctantly swallowed my pride, along with the rest of my lunch, and headed back home. My mother wisely allowed me to come to the realization, on my own, that I needed a family and a roof over my head.

The Tug-of-War between Independence and Intimacy

As much as we might rebel against it, life has a way of driving home to us the facts of our creaturely dependence and our neediness. On the one hand, we crave connection, belonging, and intimacy, but on the other hand, we hate the thought of letting go of our imagined independence, and we hate admitting that we have any needs. Often, the very people we love are the same ones we resent and react against, because we can't have it both ways. And here, exactly, is the issue: True intimacy—the blessing of knowing and being known, of being connected in healthy ways to another person instead of living in isolation and loneliness— cannot be had if we're going to insist on maintaining our absolute independence.

Intimacy means that I am giving another person access to my life, and it means they have a claim on my life and I have a claim on theirs. I am no longer completely free to go wherever I want and to do whatever I please. This is what happens—or what *should* happen—in a marriage. I give up some of my freedom in exchange for intimacy and connection. Now I *belong* to someone. It doesn't mean that the other person (whether we are talking about God or a life partner or a close friend) *controls* every detail of my life and that I cease to be responsible for my own choices and decisions. It does mean they have a claim on my life and access to it. It means that I am not my own and that there are limits to my freedom.

Intimacy with God means that I belong to Him, that I am known by Him, and that I give Him full access to my life. It means that I acknowledge my neediness, His sufficiency, my limitations, His authority. I am not going to run my own show, but instead I will walk with Him as He leads me. It means that I am His and He is mine.

To get to that point, however—to stop trying to save myself, to stop trying to protect myself, and instead to open myself to Another—requires trust; it requires risk and courage. In addition to that inborn desire to be my own god and to prove my own independence, which presents enough of a challenge by itself, there is also often a history of brokenness: broken promises, broken trust, broken relationships. We can always justify our stubborn independence by pointing to negative experiences from the past, and thus we choose to remain where we are...except that God has a better plan for each of us. Let's see how it unfolded in the life of Moses.

(By the way, now would be a good time to take ten minutes or so to familiarize yourself with Moses' backstory, by reading the first four chapters of Exodus.)

Moses' Backstory: A Life of Privilege and Pain

The story we find here is very simple and straightforward, and it's easy for us to see God's involvement in Moses' life from the moment he was born, and even in the events leading up to his birth. As Moses was growing up, however, we must remind ourselves that *he* didn't have the benefit of the perspective we have when we read the story. For him, the story was still being written, and as he grew up, he found himself in the middle of confusing and disturbing events. I'm sure he struggled with all kinds of difficult questions and conflicting emotions. He might have grown up in the lap of luxury, but it was at the same time the home of a cruel, ruthless tyrant. Let's review the main points of his story:

- The Hebrew people—the descendants of Abraham, Isaac, and Jacob—had been living in Egypt for approximately four hundred years, where they multiplied and grew into a nation, as opposed to a small minority, and yet they never assimilated.
- The ruler of Egypt felt threatened by their sheer numbers, as well as by their potential military and political power, so he decided to force them into slavery to keep them under his control.
- This plan of oppression didn't work well enough for the ruling pharaoh, so the next step was assimilation: gradually eliminating the entire Hebrew male population by killing every male that was born. Within a generation or two, the Hebrew race would have been absorbed by Egypt. Problem solved by infanticide.
- The command to throw every Hebrew baby boy into the Nile underscored the violence, cruelty, and abusive authority of this Egyptian ruler. And, of course, there was always the concentration camp–style slave labor used to grind the adult population into the ground. This man was not nice.
- In a bizarre turn of events, and thanks to a bold (and totally desperate) step of faith taken by Moses' mother and God's intervention, Moses was adopted by the pharaoh's daughter.
- After Moses was weaned (and what a great twist in the tale that Moses' own mother got *paid* by the pharaoh's daughter to nurse him!), he was taken into the Egyptian ruler's household, and this was where he grew up. God's plan to bring His people out of slavery in Egypt through the leadership of Moses had been set in motion.

Imagine what it must have been like for Moses, however. The Bible doesn't give us the details of his formative years, but when you actually reflect on the circumstances, this was not your typical family arrangement. If social media had been in existence in those days, Moses would have been hard-pressed to fill out his online profile! In the "say something about yourself" section, he probably would have given up and just written, "It's complicated." Because it really was...

On the obviously positive side, though, Moses had been rescued from almost certain death. Exodus 2:10 tells us that Pharaoh's daughter gave him the name *Moses* (which sounds like the Hebrew word for "draw out") because she had literally pulled him out of the Nile. In doing so, she had pulled him out of imminent danger, and out of a life of misery and poverty (in the unlikely event he would have even survived long enough to experience such a life).

Another hugely positive aspect of Moses' experience was the education he received. According to Acts 7:22, Moses was educated in all the learning of the Egyptians, which was considerable! He did well in his studies, and eventually became an influential person in the kingdom, as his natural leadership potential began to express itself, enabled as it was by that great education.

Now, let's consider some other things. The fact that Moses had been spared from hard labor and grew up with luxury and privilege doesn't mean that he necessarily had a smooth ride. The fact that God had a plan also doesn't mean that Moses would come through all of his experiences unscathed. It was a broken world then, and it still is today.

Growing Up under Abusive Authority

For a father figure, Moses had Pharaoh, a cruel, violent man who abused his authority and who was violently oppressing an entire people group—Moses' own people group—while he was growing up in this man's house. Moses grew up under a tyrant, and he must have witnessed injustice, outbursts of anger, and abuse on a regular basis. He might even have been the target of that abuse himself on several occasions, as most family members are when the head of the house is an angry dictator. Here are some common reactions when someone is living in such a situation:

- Simmering frustration, a heightened sensitivity to injustice, and vehement anger against that injustice. Hidden wounds lead to buried rage, which explodes when events trigger it.
- A mistrust of authority and a tendency to withdraw and protect oneself.
- A belief that "I am on my own" and that it's best that way.

Being Different

When Pharaoh's daughter pulled Moses out of the Nile, she not only pulled him out of danger, and she not only pulled him out of a life of oppression and poverty...she pulled him up out of his birth family and culture, into her own, where he would always be different and would never totally fit in. It is here that we find the roots of isolation, loneliness, and most likely a fair amount of emotional pain as the years would pass. The fact that this was all going according to God's plan would not have erased the discomfort of being different and feeling that he didn't really belong anywhere. We don't know exactly when or how Moses first became self-aware and realized that he was not like the others in his adoptive family. We don't know when he made the connection between himself and those unfortunate people who were being brutally forced to work as slaves, or how he must have struggled to reconcile these realities in his own mind. He was not Egyptian, and as time went on, he eventually decided he didn't want to identity with the Egyptians. Hebrews 11:24–25 tells us that at some point Moses made a conscious choice: He refused to be called the son of Pharaoh's daughter any longer. He renounced a life of luxury and privilege and instead chose to identify with the Hebrew people in their suffering. But as the story progresses, we see that he was not so easily accepted by the Hebrews, either, who were sure to mistrust this man who had grown up in the Egyptian ruler's household.

Running Away

When Moses was forty years old, a lifetime of living under abusive, unjust authority and a lifetime of being different came together in the perfect storm. Within the space of two days, events conspired to send Moses into forty years of self-imposed exile.

He was moved by the concern for his fellow Hebrews and so he set out to see for himself what was happening outside of the palace walls. What was happening was that a Hebrew slave was being cruelly beaten by an Egyptian foreman. It was too much; the anger and frustration over all of the injustice that had been building up over a lifetime erupted in that single moment. With a quick glance to the right and left to make sure no one was watching, Moses killed the Egyptian on the spot and buried his body in the sand. He probably felt immense relief, and he probably assumed also that this would win him acceptance with his own people.

He was wrong.

The next day, Moses was out there again, and when he tried to intervene once more—this time to stop a fight between two Hebrews—he got a nasty surprise. The aggressor stuck his chin out, got in Moses' face, and in a voice that was seething with contempt, said, "Who made you the judge, huh? Where do you get the authority to stick your nose into our business? Are you going to kill me like you killed the Egyptian yesterday?" Moses got the message loud and clear: *We don't want you, we don't trust you, and we don't need you here! You're not one of us.* It was a cruel shock, especially when he was thinking he had finally found his place. That rejection, along with word having gotten out about the previous day's activities—apparently his own newly adopted people had betrayed him to the Egyptians—sealed Moses' decision to run away from it all and to never get involved again. It just wasn't worth the trouble!

A Nice Quiet Corner of the World

Moses fled to Midian. This place was really out in the sticks, apparently a small rural community with more livestock than people, which suited Moses just fine. He sat down by a well. Even there, however, injustice was happening! Seven daughters of a priest came along with their father's flocks and drew enough water to fill all the troughs so that the animals could drink—not a small task. Moses could have lent a hand, but he reminded himself instead that he wasn't getting involved, that it was safer that way. After all, these girls had been doing this task on a daily basis long before he showed up, he might have reasoned. "They don't need me, and I am NOT getting involved... I'm not!" But then, just as they'd finished drawing and hauling this huge amount of water, the local gang of shepherds arrived and they decided to take advantage of the full watering troughs for their own livestock, chasing the sisters away like the typical bullies they were. Moses just couldn't help himself. Hardly before he even knew what he was doing, he rescued the girls and put the ill-mannered bad boys in their place.

Things went better here in Midian than they had during his last attempt to save the day, back in Egypt. In this little community, sticking up for the girls won Moses the approval of their father, one of the daughters as his wife, and a place—hidden away as it was—among the locals. It won him a quiet life of detachment with few demands, few commitments, and the freedom to do as he pleased—not that there was a lot to do. It was perfect. It was so perfect that he stayed there for the next forty years.

But even in Midian, safely insulated from the world, Moses would maintain a certain distance between himself and the community where he was living. The naming of his firstborn son is indicative of his new approach to life: **Gershom** means "sojourner." A stranger, a visitor, rather than a full member of the community. It was best to remain uncommitted, comfortably independent, and not risk giving too much of himself away.

Now, before we reach the big turning point in Moses' story, let's take a moment to reflect on your own story. Is this how you have decided to live out your days, safely insulated from the risky business of getting involved? Maybe way-back-when, you had high hopes of doing good and making a difference, of being a part of something grand, but things didn't turn out like you expected. Maybe you encountered misunderstanding, rejection, conflicts you never could have imagined. After the initial hurt subsided to a dull ache, you found yourself in the gray atmosphere of disappointment—maybe even disappointment with God—wondering what just happened. Eventually you found an emotional and relational "safe zone," where you've managed to carve out a "normal" life for yourself. "So, what's wrong with that?" you may ask. What's wrong with it is this: **You are depriving the world of gifts and graces and the glory of God that He wants to express uniquely through you, and you are robbing yourself of the deep friendship with God that you were created to experience.**

When we insulate ourselves from other people and from the risk of being hurt by them, we also insulate ourselves against intimacy with God, who will always seek to take us beyond our safe zones so that we can grow in trust and intimacy.

Now, let's get back to Moses' story.

The Invitation and the Challenge

Even after the long space of forty years, Moses showed no signs of wanting to return to Egypt or to involve himself again in the affairs of the people whom he had left behind. It was just another day of the simple life, until one day...

> Moses was tending the flock of Jethro his father-in-law, the priest of Midian, and he led the flock to the far side of the wilderness and came to Horeb, the mountain of God. There the angel of the Lord appeared to him in flames of fire from within a bush. Moses saw that though the bush was on fire it did not burn up. So Moses thought, "I will go over and see this strange sight—why the bush does not burn up."
> When the Lord saw that he had gone over to look, God called to him from within the bush, "Moses! Moses!"
> And Moses said, "Here I am" (Exodus 3:1–4).

What began as a normal day, in familiar, safe surroundings, became an extraordinary turning point for Moses, a turning point from which he was propelled into one of the most amazing adventures the world has ever known. God spoke clearly, Moses argued desperately, and the world was about to be changed. Here's how it unfolded...

Moses was doing what he had been doing every day for presumably a very long time, but something interrupted this comfortable monotony to catch his attention. He didn't seem to realize that he was about to be ambushed by the Lord, who had decided it was time. God called to Moses from the burning bush, and Moses' "here I am" was more of an automatic response than a careful and deliberate one. Now, here's the confusing part: God had just called to Moses, but as Moses began to approach, he was stopped in his tracks.

> "Do not come any closer," God said. "Take off your sandals, for the place where you are standing is holy ground." Then he said, "I am the God of your father, the God of Abraham, the God of Isaac and the God of Jacob." At this, Moses hid his face, because he was afraid to look at God" (Exodus 3:5–6).

Why? Why couldn't Moses come any closer unless he took off his sandals? Were his shoes somehow offensive to God? Was it the sheep dung that had probably dried onto the bottom of those well-worn sandals? As I've read and pondered the rest of the story, I've come to the conclusion that dirt has nothing to do with it. Here's what I believe is really going on: The terrain where Moses found himself was harsh, rocky desert terrain, full of sharp stones, pebbles, and scrubby thorn bushes, very similar to the terrain of my mission base in Mali, West Africa. Without shoes, it's impossible to go very far, and you're definitely not going to run anywhere! Based on the prolonged exchange that followed between the Lord and Moses (read Exodus 3:6–4:17), after he had complied with the Lord's instructions and removed his sandals, I believe that if Moses *could* have run away, he would have. God was sending him *back* to everything he had run away from forty years earlier—and Moses was not exactly thrilled at the prospect. But since he had taken off his sandals and left them some distance away from the bush, he stayed, he listened, and he eventually surrendered to the Lord's plan—which would mean that his days of isolation and independence were finally over.

To put it simply and directly, in commanding Moses to take off his sandals, **God was challenging him to give up his right to run away**. This was the demand, the nonnegotiable condition of intimacy. It's the challenge to lay aside our stubborn independence, that "right" we have reserved for ourselves to run away or withdraw from the from the place where God has positioned us, when we don't like it anymore. This self-protective, independent mindset is possibly the most common barrier to greater intimacy with God the Father and deeper relationships with others. From this pivotal moment, when Moses took off his sandals and laid aside his self-protective independence, he was launched on a journey that ultimately brought him into deep, soul-transforming friendship with God. It's important to note that in all of the Lord's reassurances to Moses, He never promised that Moses would not be hurt, or misunderstood, or rejected ever again. His promise was much better—and it is one that addresses all of our needs too, at the deepest levels. The Lord simply said, "**I will be with you.**" These five simple words are the promise of the Father's personal, solid, and reassuring **presence**; this is the promise of intimacy—if we will surrender our independence. This is where the journey truly begins.

He Doesn't Want You to Go It Alone

There are a few other important things I want us to note as we consider Moses, and how he proceeded from this point on. The plan was not only that Moses would set out on a journey to intimacy with God for himself, but the Lord intended that he would bring a few others along with him on the adventure—about a million or two, actually, constituting the entire fledgling Hebrew nation. Before that could happen, however, **before he could move forward, Moses had to go back** to face the very things from which he had fled all those years ago—the abusive authority, the rejection he had endured from his own people, and the experiences that had so shattered him. But this time, it would be different, because he would not face these things in his own strength or with his old, brash self-confidence, but he would face them with the promise and the presence of the Lord, who had pledged to be with him. He would go in humble **dependence**—and not only dependence on God, *but dependence on a flesh-and-blood brother, Aaron.*

> But Moses said, "Pardon your servant, Lord. Please send someone else."
> Then the Lord's anger burned against Moses and he said, "What about your brother, Aaron the Levite? I know he can speak well. He is already on his way to meet you, and he will be glad to see you. You shall speak to him and put words in his mouth; I will help both of you speak and will teach you what to do" (Exodus 4:13–15).

After Moses had produced every possible concern, objection, and excuse he could think of, and after the Lord had patiently answered each one in turn (even throwing in a few supernatural signs meant to erase all doubt), this reluctant prophet still made one last-ditch attempt to refuse—a telling example of just how deep our stubborn, self-protective independence is often rooted. But forty years had been long enough for Moses to live this way, the time had finally come, and the plan had already been set in motion. So often, our subtle, or not-so-subtle, negotiations with God are simply a measure of our unwillingness to trust and acknowledge that He must be in control—not us! It's all about who's in charge. God's stubbornness—which is really His great faithfulness—can outlast ours any day of the week! So, the Lord said, "Enough! I'm sending you and that's that! But you're not going to do this alone. I've already made arrangements, and your brother, Aaron, is already on his way to meet you." And then we see this sweet detail: "**And he will be glad to see you.**" Even in His anger, the Lord is so kind. The first person whom Moses is going to meet, the one who would become his right-hand man, would not be suspicious, angry, or difficult. He would welcome Moses with open arms and an open heart. It will always be true that "it is not good for man to be alone," and none of us is meant to undertake this journey by ourselves.

In order to move forward, you may need to go back and revisit some painful experiences that have seemingly crippled you, just like Moses had to, because the Father wants you to overcome them. He wants you to realize that you are not facing those things alone, but that He is holding your hand. When you do, you will find that He was there all along, and that He can take all the pain of the past and turn it into something good for the future, something powerful. The Father will bring others alongside of you to walk with you as you surrender independence for intimacy, and isolation for connection. Your brothers and sisters are already out there, and they'll be glad to see you coming their way. It's His way, because a Father creates a family.

There's a poisonous, persistent lie that is prevalent among believers, that we should all be able to "get it together," to get the victory, to overcome our sins and problems, and to work it out, just between us and the Lord—that we shouldn't need any help from other human beings. The idea persists that if we can't get it together on our own, we're somehow inferior, deficient, and lacking in faith. This is bad theology that was started by Satan himself, when he enticed Adam and Eve to reject creaturely dependence on God and one another and to become their own gods; we've been hiding in separate corners ever since. "Do-it-yourself" is not noble, it's not spiritual or commendable, it's a lie! It's a lie that we sometimes spiritualize and prefer because of pride, shame, and the fear of letting others in. But connection is the Father's way, and intimacy is far better than independence. It's time to lay down the excuses and start the journey.

6

The Breaking of a Good Man: Peter's Story

Simon, also called Peter, which means "rock" (a name given to him by Jesus Himself), was definitely not someone who struggled with self-doubt or a lack of confidence. He was one of the trio who made up Jesus' inner circle, which also included James and John, those guys who had been nicknamed the "sons of thunder." I wonder how they earned that label? Peter himself was a rugged, hardworking fisherman, a natural-born leader who never seemed afraid to speak up or to jump into a situation and take action. He lacked the polish of any formal education or training, and he was often clumsy and brash, but he made up for it with his sincerity, his passion, and his wholehearted commitment. From the moment he responded to Jesus' call to leave his fishing nets and follow Him, he was all-in.

As far as we can tell from the gospel accounts, it doesn't seem that Peter had experienced any crippling wounds in his past, any breaking points that would have inclined him to retreat into self-protection. Rather than withdraw from life and keep his distance, like Moses did in our last chapter, Peter seemed always ready to jump in feet-first. Here's what I mean:

Immediately Jesus made the disciples get into the boat and go on ahead of him to the other side, while he dismissed the crowd. After he had dismissed them, he went up on a mountainside by himself to pray. Later that night, he was there alone, and the boat was already a considerable distance from land, buffeted by the waves because the wind was against it.

Shortly before dawn Jesus went out to them, walking on the lake. When the disciples saw him walking on the lake, they were terrified. "It's a ghost," they said, and cried out in fear. But Jesus immediately said to them: "Take courage! It is I. Don't be afraid."

"Lord, if it's you," Peter replied, "tell me to come to you on the water."

"Come," he said.

Then Peter got down out of the boat, walked on the water and came toward Jesus. But when he saw the wind, he was afraid and, beginning to sink, cried out, "Lord, save me!"

Immediately Jesus reached out his hand and caught him. "You of little faith," he said, "why did you doubt?" (Matthew 14:22–31).

No one but Peter would have done something so daring! His faith might have been small, but he did something with it that the other men in that boat would never have thought to do! In his unbridled self-confidence, Peter was frequently the first to speak and the first to act—whether or not he understood the situation in which he found himself. He assumed that something had to be said or done, and he was usually the one to say it or do it. His sincerity is never in doubt throughout the Scriptures, but sheer boldness and a strong personality (what we would call a "type-A personality") aren't necessarily the one-size-fits-all answer to every challenge. Still, Peter and those like him tend to assume they already know the answers and that it's up to them to step in and do something, since no one else seems to get it or step up to the plate! Consider the following scenarios...

> From that time on Jesus began to explain to his disciples that he must go to Jerusalem and suffer many things at the hands of the elders, the chief priests and the teachers of the law, and that he must be killed and on the third day be raised to life. Peter took him aside and began to rebuke him.
> "Never, Lord!" he said. "This shall never happen to you!"
> Jesus turned and said to Peter,
> "Get behind me, Satan! You are a stumbling block to me; you do not have in mind the concerns of God, but merely human concerns" (Matthew 16:21–23).

Peter had just had a revelation about who Jesus really was—the chosen Messiah and Son of God. He was ready to run with that revelation, assuming he already knew how the rest of the story should go. He had no idea how far off-base he was, and he received a stern rebuke from Jesus. But he still didn't know what he didn't know... Consider this solemn, intimate scene in the Upper Room as Jesus prepared His disciples for what was coming:

> He came to Simon Peter, who said to him, "Lord, are you going to wash my feet?"
> Jesus replied, "You do not realize now what I am doing, but later you will understand."
> "No," said Peter, "you shall never wash my feet."
> Jesus answered, "Unless I wash you, you have no part with me."
> "Then, Lord," Simon Peter replied, "not just my feet but my hands and my head as well!"

> Jesus answered, "Those who have had a bath need only to wash their feet; their whole body is clean. And you are clean, though not every one of you." For he knew who was going to betray him, and that was why he said not every one was clean" (John 14:6–11).

Here again, without fully understanding the gravity of the moment, Peter was attempting to take the lead and to tell Jesus how things should go.

Here's one more classic "Peter" move, which took place during Jesus' arrest in the Garden of Gethsemane:

> Again he [Jesus] asked them, "Who is it you want?"
> "Jesus of Nazareth," they said.
> Jesus answered, "I told you that I am he. If you are looking for me, then let these men go." This happened so that the words he had spoken would be fulfilled: "I have not lost one of those you gave me."
> Then Simon Peter, who had a sword, drew it and struck the high priest's servant, cutting off his right ear. (The servant's name was Malchus.)
> Jesus commanded Peter, "Put your sword away! Shall I not drink the cup the Father has given me?" (John 18:7–11).

I'm sure you get the picture at this point. Peter's confidence in himself was apparently boundless, and he didn't understand the reality of his own weakness (which was going to be exposed in spectacular fashion before it was all over). You may be wondering, *But what does all this have to do with the struggle between independence and intimacy?* By the end of Peter's story, I think it will be clear. For now, I will just say that **intimacy with God requires that we give up control**—that we stop living by our own strength, that we stop following our own assumptions, and that we stop running our own show. The Bible calls this relinquishment of control humility, and we can't get very far without it, since God resists the proud but gives grace to the humble.

You're Going to Fall, but It Will Be Okay

"You will all fall away," Jesus told them, "for it is written:

"'I will strike the shepherd, and the sheep will be scattered.' But after I have risen, I will go ahead of you into Galilee."

Peter declared, "Even if all fall away, I will not."

"Truly I tell you," Jesus answered, "today—yes, tonight—before the rooster crows twice you yourself will disown me three times."

But Peter insisted emphatically, "Even if I have to die with you, I will never disown you." And all the others said the same. (Mark 14:27-31)

"My children, I will be with you only a little longer. You will look for me, and just as I told the Jews, so I tell you now: Where I am going, you cannot come. A new command I give you: Love one another. As I have loved you, so you must love one another. By this everyone will know that you are my disciples, if you love one another."

Simon Peter asked him, "Lord, where are you going?"

Jesus replied, "Where I am going, you cannot follow now, but you will follow later."

Peter asked, "Lord, why can't I follow you now? I will lay down my life for you."

Then Jesus answered, "Will you really lay down your life for me? Very truly I tell you, before the rooster crows, you will disown me three times!

"Do not let your hearts be troubled. You believe in God; believe also in me. My Father's house has many rooms; if that were not so, would I have told you that I am going there to prepare a place for you? And if I go and prepare a place for you, I will come back and take you **to be with me that you also may be where I am.** You know the way to the place where I am going." (John 13:33 - 4:4)

From the start, Peter had been part of Jesus' inner circle. Along with James and John, he had been included in some of the most powerful encounters and intimate moments of the Lord's three and a half years of ministry—*but yet he often missed the point and failed to see beyond the surface to receive Jesus' self-revelation in those moments.* He was more focused on the "success" of the enterprise and what he could do to ensure that success (especially as Jesus' most dedicated disciple—in his own mind at least), and so he failed to experience the intimacy that was being offered. It's hard to experience intimacy in relationships when you've always got something to prove. But now Jesus was going away, and this time the disciples couldn't follow—*not even Peter.* He couldn't accept that there was something he was not capable of doing, especially when it was the most important thing of all. Observe in Mark's account of the Upper Room scene how Peter essentially claimed to be the most dedicated disciple: "**Even if all fall away,** I will not!" I wonder how the other disciples felt about that statement? I'm sure Peter's heart sank like a stone when Jesus looked at him and said, "No, Peter, not only are you incapable of following Me right now, but you're going to fall flat on your face just trying!" Imagine yourself in Peter's place. After all this time working your hardest, trying your utmost to prove your worth, to be the best, Jesus has just told you that you would fail—and fail badly! You would feel sick with dismay and disbelief. But then, in His very next breath, He said the craziest thing: "**Don't worry about it—it's going to be okay**. Trust God, and trust Me! (Maybe as opposed to trusting in your own ability get everything right). I'm going to do something for you, something that will make it possible for you to follow Me and to be with Me—really be **with me**—where I am. I'm going to bring you to a place of intimacy you could never get to on your own!"

As that night progressed, events unfolded just as Jesus predicted. When He was arrested and taken to the residence of the high priest, Peter and John followed at a distance. John was somehow already known to the high priest's family, so he went in, but Peter had to wait at the gate until John came back out to vouch for him. And this was where Peter's bold claims—that he would follow Jesus to the end and never falter—pitifully unraveled. A servant girl, the most unimportant person imaginable in that day, was on-duty at the gate. And suddenly all of Peter's bold self-confidence, all of his formidable self-strength, crumbled in that moment as she challenged him with the question: "You aren't one of this man's disciples too, are you?"

"**I am not!**" All the hidden fear, all the human weakness that he could never acknowledge, betrayed him in that moment, and he couldn't stand up to even a young teenage girl—let alone the men who would question him a second and third time as they all stood around a charcoal fire to stay warm. He would make the same denial at each challenge, finally with some angry curses thrown in for good measure. He would come to intimately understand the reality of his weakness as a man, the limits of his own ability. The Scripture tells us that after that took place, he went out and wept bitterly. My guess is that he was not only weeping over the fact that he had publicly disowned the dearest Friend a man could ever have, but he was equally weeping over the shattering of that false but cherished self-image he had held as the strongest, the best, the most devoted disciple. When that image you've lovingly polished and protected lies in pieces around you and you are brought to realize that you've done no better than anyone else—and possibly much worse—it's a bitter moment indeed. But it's also a blessed one. It was by far the worst thing and, at the same time, the best thing that could have happened to Peter. That native independence, born of a naïve trust in his own abilities, was finally crumbling.

Follow Me—Intimacy through Obedience

If you've read the gospel accounts, you know the rest of the story. In the days following Jesus' resurrection, He appeared to the group of disciples on several occasions with words of peace, reassurance, and the hope of good things to come. Beneath the mind-blowing joy they must have experienced, however, I wonder what was going on in Peter's heart and mind. From the confusion of Jesus' arrest in the Garden of Gethsemane, where "they all left Him and fled," to Peter's pivotal failure in the courtyard of the high priest, none of them had exactly been star performers! The private conversations Jesus must have had with the disciples after His resurrection are not recorded for us (and I like that fact, actually!), but this "in-between time" had to have been somewhat awkward while everyone waited for whatever was coming next. You see, there was an "elephant in the room"—Peter's profanity-laced denial of Jesus—which no one was talking about. Peter must have been wondering if things could ever be the same between him and the Lord—but Jesus had a plan. And no, this relationship would never be the same. It would actually be better and deeper than ever before.

Finally the day came for a "reboot" of Peter's relationship with Jesus, the day to clear the air and to begin again. Take a few moments to read about it in John 21:

Afterward Jesus appeared again to his disciples, by the Sea of Galilee. It happened this way: Simon Peter, Thomas (also known as Didymus), Nathanael from Cana in Galilee, the sons of Zebedee, and two other disciples were together. "I'm going out to fish," Simon Peter told them, and they said, "We'll go with you." So they went out and got into the boat, but that night they caught nothing.

Early in the morning, Jesus stood on the shore, but the disciples did not realize that it was Jesus. He called out to them, "Friends, haven't you any fish?"
"No," they answered.
He said, "Throw your net on the right side of the boat and you will find some." When they did, they were unable to haul the net in because of the large number of fish.

Then the disciple whom Jesus loved said to Peter, "It is the Lord!" As soon as Simon Peter heard him say, "It is the Lord," he wrapped his outer garment around him (for he had taken it off) and jumped into the water. The other disciples followed in the boat, towing the net full of fish, for they were not far from shore, about a hundred yards. When they landed, they saw a fire of burning coals there with fish on it, and some bread.

Jesus said to them, "Bring some of the fish you have just caught." So Simon Peter climbed back into the boat and dragged the net ashore. It was full of large fish,

153, but even with so many the net was not torn. Jesus said to them, "Come and have breakfast." None of the disciples dared ask him, "Who are you?" They knew it was the Lord. Jesus came, took the bread and gave it to them, and did the same with the fish. This was now the third time Jesus appeared to his disciples after he was raised from the dead.

When they had finished eating, Jesus said to Simon Peter, "Simon son of John, do you love me more than these?"
"Yes, Lord," he said, "you know that I love you."
Jesus said, "Feed my lambs."
Again Jesus said, "Simon son of John, do you love me?"
He answered, "Yes, Lord, you know that I love you."
Jesus said, "Take care of my sheep."
The third time he said to him, "Simon son of John, do you love me?"

Peter was hurt because Jesus asked him the third time, "Do you love me?" He said, "Lord, you know all things; you know that I love you."
Jesus said, "Feed my sheep. **Very truly I tell you, when you were younger you dressed yourself and went where you wanted; but when you are old you will stretch out your hands, and someone else will dress you and lead you where you do not want to go.**" Jesus said this to indicate the kind of death by which Peter would glorify God. Then he said to him, "Follow me!"
Peter turned and saw that the disciple whom Jesus loved was following them. (This was the one who had leaned back against Jesus at the supper and had said, "Lord, who is going to betray you?") When Peter saw him, he asked, "Lord, what about him?"

Jesus answered, "If I want him to remain alive until I
return, what is that to you? **You must follow me.**"

Peter's journey with Jesus had begun several years before with
a very similar event, after he had fished all night with his com-
panions and caught nothing, but then after following Jesus' instructions, he had put down the nets one more time and hauled
in a huge catch. At that time, he was overwhelmed with the realization of his own weakness and Jesus' supreme ability and authority, and he humbled himself. (See Luke 5:1–11.) Jesus' response was simply, "Don't be afraid!" with an invitation to follow
Him. So maybe this scene in John 21 signaled a new beginning
for Peter, another chance to leave behind his own way of doing
things through brash self-confidence, and to become a trusting,
obedient follower submitted to the Father's will.

I love the way Jesus confronted and restored Peter as they all
sat around a charcoal fire on the beach. It was simple, it was
kind, and it cut right to the heart of the matter. There was no
formal inquisition in front of a tribunal to rehearse Peter's failure, to underscore how terrible it was. Just a conversation that
took place in a circle of intimate friends, dealing with matters of
the heart. "Peter, do you love Me **more than these?**" Remember
Peter's confident boast—that even if everyone else fell away, he
would still be right there at Jesus' side? There's no boast now,
just a humble, sincere, "Yes, Lord, You know that I love You."
He didn't add anything to it, no big claims, no declarations of
the great things he was going to do or the impressive plans he
had. Peter finally understood his own weakness, his capacity for
failure, and his deep need. From that day on, he was letting Jesus
take the lead and set the agenda.

Twice more, the same question, until Peter's heart was sore.
But this question was the only one that really mattered. Love. It

means we're not free to do our own thing, run our own show, and go our own way. That independent way of life and those days of immaturity must be left behind; things are different now. Love binds us to the Beloved, to His agenda, His people, His priorities. **This is the intimacy of obedience.** The command that Jesus attaches to love is the command to serve, to take care of others for His sake, rather than to chase greatness in an attempt to prove our own ability and worth.

Jesus' final words to Peter in this chapter may sound ominous, this contrast between when he was younger, when he did what he wanted and went where he pleased, and the future, when he would abandon his freedom utterly for the sake of love—even to the point of death. But the reward was intimate fellowship with Jesus, and so one last time, the invitation came with the force of a command: "Follow Me!"

There is a daily choice set before us between the independence of self-sufficiency (which is so admired in this world), and that special fellowship with God that we can only experience through humility, dependence, and obedience. And this is the one thing that will truly satisfy our souls.

7

The Struggle for Identity: The Father's Design and Your True Name

For you created my inmost being
you knit me together in my mother's womb.
I praise you because I am fearfully and wonderfully made;
your works are wonderful, I know that full well.
My frame was not hidden from you when I was made in the secret place,
when I was woven together in the depths of the earth.
Your eyes saw my unformed body; all the days ordained for me were written in your book before one of them came to be. (Psalms 139:13-16).

For this reason I kneel before the Father, from whom every family in heaven and on earth derives its name. (Ephesians 3:14-15).

"Whoever has ears, let them hear what the Spirit says to the churches. To the one who is victorious, I will

give some of the hidden manna. I will also give that person a white stone with a new name written on it, known only to the one who receives it."
(Revelation 2:17).

"I hate how I don't feel real enough unless people are watching."
—Chuck Palahniuk, Invisible Monsters

"When I discover who I am, I'll be free."
— Ralph Ellison, Invisible Man

"Most people are other people. Their thoughts are someone else's opinions, their lives a mimicry, their passions a quotation."
— Oscar Wilde

It had been a long return trip from the Democratic Republic of Congo, where I had accompanied our organization's president to serve as his interpreter, and I wasn't home yet. Going through Immigration at Logan International Airport in Boston, I felt slightly uncomfortable as the agent seemed to scrutinize my passport, and me, beyond the minute or less it usually takes (or used to take, in pre–9/11 America). And although he eventually waved me through, it was not with the usual "Welcome home, Mr. Butler." But I had no inkling of any real problem until we retrieved our things from baggage claim and handed our customs forms to the agent manning that post. After demanding our passports, frowning several times while glancing rapidly back and forth between the documents and our faces, he walked away abruptly and left us standing there for what seemed like ages. I don't like it when someone I don't know walks away with my passport—my only solid proof of identity until I am officially admitted back into my own country. After an interval during which time seemed to stand still— even though the minutes continued to pass and my connecting flight to Baltimore would leave whether I was on it or not—another official appeared. Then the rapid-fire questions began.

"Where were you? What were you doing there? Did you engage in business, make money? Did you bring money back with you? Why is he [pointing to our organization's president, who is severely vision-impaired and was sticking close to me until his own connecting flight] going to Rochester and you're going to Baltimore?"

"Um...because I live there."

"Kinshasa?"

"Um, no. Baltimore."

I couldn't imagine what was going on. "Wait here," we were told. Another space of time passed, during which my hopes of making my connecting flight began to dwindle. Eventually the first official returned, handed us our passports, and told us we were free to go. There was no explanation, and my only focus now was to recheck my bags and get to the gate for my flight to Baltimore as quickly as possible. I managed to get on the flight, but my bags were not so lucky. They arrived at my house a day later—with some damage. I was annoyed about the whole incident, so I tracked down the phone number for Customs and Immigration at Logan Airport and voiced my complaint. To my amazement, I actually did get an explanation! It turns out that the FBI had issued an All-Points Bulletin for someone named Paul Butler, who was wanted for several crimes. *This individual not only had my name, but he was also apparently about the same age, height and build as me*, so of course the officials at the airport had to make sure that I wasn't him!

It was a bit unsettling to learn that someone with my name, someone who could be mistaken for me—or I for him!—was out there somewhere committing serious crimes. I never had a moment of doubt about my own identity, but the airport officials sure did, so they had to check things out. It turns out that I share the name Paul Butler with more than a few people in this world, something I discovered when I joined Facebook years ago and was promptly invited to join a group called "We Are Paul Butler." Go figure! I made at least one good friendship out of that group that continues to this day, but beyond sharing the same name, we are all very different from one another. Identity is far deeper than a given name on a legal document.

The Bible says that it is from the Father "that every family in heaven and on earth derives its name" (Ephesians 3:14–15). The word *name* usually stands for identity—the true character and essence of a person—in biblical language. So, in other words, your true identity is determined by the One who crafted you uniquely in His image and who breathed you into existence. It is impossible to arrive at a healthy and true sense of self while living in a state of disconnection from the original Self—the "I AM" who has identified himself to us as *the Father*, and from whom we derive our very being.

Though we all share some of the physical characteristics—and maybe even some of the personality traits—of our parents and siblings, each of us is entirely unique and created by God to do His will and to reflect His glory and goodness on the earth in a way that no one else can. I know that some of us have a hard time believing that, but the truth is that your uniqueness, your true identity, is not only good; it's powerful and brimming with history-changing potential! This is exactly why Satan works so hard to squash it, to erase it, to ridicule and obscure the real you.

He works to rob us of our God-ordained identity. The battle is fierce, and his tactics are vicious.

In the Father's great plan, conceived in perfect love, it is **human beings** who are His image-bearers—*not* angels. Though we are made of dust, we who are flesh and blood are also indelibly stamped with the very image of God and are created to enjoy a familial relationship with Him that angels can never fathom. The Bible tells us that the angels are ministering spirits created to serve this divine family (see Hebrews 1:4–14). I believe Satan has always been jealous of our status as sons and daughters who are God's image-bearers. As we have already seen in Genesis 3, Satan's tactic to separate Adam and Eve from the Father was not only meant to cast doubt on God's goodness, but also to attack and belittle their own identity and status as those made in God's image: "If you listen to me, then your eyes will really be opened, then you'll be **like God**." In those fateful moments, they somehow forgot that they already were like God, they forgot the Source of their very identity, and they traded that original glory for a lie. In all the years since, not much has changed. The struggle is described for us so well in Romans 1:

> For although they knew God, they neither glorified him as God nor gave thanks to him, but their thinking became futile and their foolish hearts were darkened. Although they claimed to be wise, they became fools and exchanged the glory of the immortal God for images made to look like a mortal human beings and birds and animals and reptiles. Therefore God gave them over in the sinful desires of their hearts to sexual impurity for the degrading of their bodies with one another. They exchanged the truth about God for a lie, and worshiped and served created things rather than

the Creator—who is forever praised. Amen (Romans 1:21–25).

What I want to point out here is this fatal exchange: **"They exchanged the glory of the immortal God for images...** they exchanged the truth for a lie... and they served created things rather than the Creator."** Our world today is all about **images**; they are pervasive and powerful. The primary means of influence in Western society today is images, and many of these images are, in biblical terms, ''lying images.'' They are relentlessly shoved in our faces at every turn—images that tell us who we should be, what we should aspire to, how we should look, what we must wear to be acceptable, likable, worthy human beings. There is constant pressure to bow down and conform—as impossible as it may be—to these images of beauty and success. Once again, Satan offers us an identity to chase after, all the while mocking us because we will never have that perfect smile, that flawless face, that sculpted body. We'll never belong to that trendy circle of beautiful people... These seductive images are a fantasy—mirages with no substance behind them. And all the while, we are losing ourselves and falling short of that original glory as we look to created things to tell us who we should be, instead of looking to the Father and Creator who is the very Source of our existence and identity. He alone, and no one else, has the right to give to each of us our true name.

Recorded for us in the Bible are stories of several people who experienced a name change, who had liberating encounters with God and came out on the other side of those encounters as their **true selves.**

One of those people was Jacob, who was ultimately given a new name: Israel. It is from this man that an entire nation took its name, a nation whose identity—like their forefathers'—was

THE GOOD FATHER • 109

meant to be shaped by God Himself rather than by the prevailing culture and the influences of the world around it. But the tug-of-war between these competing forces is intense, and even today we are caught in the struggle—which is exactly why Jacob's story is so powerful and has so many lessons for us. Jacob struggled fiercely, bitterly and for many years, to discover and accept his true identity. He fought desperately to achieve what God had planned to give him all along, and more often than not he was fighting the very One who had destined him for blessing and honor.

There is no reason for me to retell a story here that is already told superbly in the Scriptures, so now would be a good time for you to read Jacob's story as it is found in **Genesis 25:19–34; chapters 27, 28, 29, and chapter 30, beginning with verse 25, through chapter 32.** I know this may seem like a lot of Bible chapters to read in one sitting, but I guarantee that the story is a real page-turner and you'll be hooked from the start! I'm going to summarize the main points of the story here (kind of like *CliffsNotes*) for the sake of clarity and simplicity, but trust me, you'll get lots more out of this if you read Jacob's saga for yourself in its entirety.

Jacob: Chosen by God (but Ignored by Dad)

Here is a brief summary of Jacob's story. (I'm skipping over volumes of stuff that is full of powerful life lessons, but we could never cover it all in this chapter.)

- God chose Jacob before he was born. See Genesis 25:19–34.
- Jacob's father, Isaac, didn't value him or choose him. His older brother, Esau, was a rugged "man's man," the traditional model of manhood that their father valued and preferred. Here is the root of rejection and unbelief: Jacob

could not believe he was chosen by God since he hadn't ever been valued or chosen by his father. See Genesis 25:27–29.

- Jacob desperately wanted his father's blessing and approval. See Genesis 25:29–34; 27 (the whole chapter).
- Jacob became someone he was not (he took on a false identity) in order to get that approval. He didn't know or couldn't believe that God had planned to bless him greatly from the beginning. He thought that fighting and scheming was the only way. See Genesis 27:14–25.
- Jacob became a practiced schemer and fighter, always striving and manipulating people and circumstances to get hold of the blessing (which in his mind was material wealth, success, and supremacy over others). **This is an exhausting, insecure way to live.** See Genesis chapters 29 to 31.
- After many years, God forced Jacob to give up his struggle for success and control and brought him to a place of surrender. God literally wrestled him to the ground—not to punish him, but so that He could bless him directly, deliberately, and face-to-face! See Genesis 32:22–26.
- In this place of confrontation and surrender, Jacob received his true name and identity: Israel, meaning "prince of God." See Genesis 32:27–32.

A Divine Plan and a Dysfunctional Family

Reading through the book of Genesis, it doesn't take long to realize that the families of the patriarchs—Abraham, Isaac, and Jacob—were not exactly models of healthy relationships. You probably shouldn't take your cue from these Old Testament saints when it comes to marriage and family issues. And whatever you do, if you're a parent, don't take any parenting tips from Isaac or Rebekah!

Although Esau and Jacob were twins, they could not have been more different from one another. Even before their birth, it seems they were in a wrestling match for supremacy. In response to Rebekah's concerns, the Lord told her that she was carrying the founders of two nations—two powerful, forceful individuals—but that the younger would ultimately come out on top as the leader. Of course, from the day of their birth, when Esau, red and hairy all over, came out first and then Jacob followed, smooth-skinned but with a strong grip on his brother's heel, she knew. As the boys grew, their parents fell into a pattern that was sure to produce problems:

> The boys grew up, and Esau became a skillful hunter, a man of the open country, while Jacob was content to stay at home among the tents. **Isaac, who had a taste for wild game, loved Esau, but Rebekah loved Jacob** (Gen. 25:27–28).

Openly preferring one child over the other did more harm to the family unit—and to all the individuals involved—than either Isaac or Rebekah could have foreseen. There was a tragic division as each parent aligned themselves with their favorite son, which left Isaac and Rebekah working at cross purposes instead of in unity. It caused Isaac to turn a blind eye to the moral failings and ungodly character of his older son, Esau, who lived to satisfy his physical cravings, and to virtually ignore his younger son, Jacob, who would have craved his father's notice and approval. Because of personal preference, Isaac became blind to God's will concerning his sons.

As for Rebekah, she became an expert manipulator of people and situations, assuming that God's plan needed her interference to come to fruition. She interfered in the lives of her sons to such a degree that she lost both of them, and it was only after her death that they ever reconciled.

As for both Jacob and Esau, their stories indicate that each of them experienced a painful sense of rejection—the exact opposite of what their parents intended—and of course, each of them developed destructive ways of handling that rejection. (See Genesis 25:29–34.) The good news here is that the God of grace, our good Father, was at work even in the middle of all the mess and dysfunction to redeem, to restore, and to accomplish His good plan. Jacob, however, was definitely going to take a long, difficult road to arrive at that realization.

Rejection: The Harder You Try, the Worse It Gets...

Have you ever been involved in one of those family dramas that is so hurtful, so shocking or traumatic, that you truly wish it had never happened, that you could erase all memory of it—the kind of experience that leaves you feeling as if a bomb went off and there's no possible way to repair all the damage? That's how Genesis 27 feels to me. On the surface, it seems a bit comical as Jacob pitifully impersonates his older brother, but overall the shame and tragedy, the sheer lowness of this debacle, make it uncomfortable to read—a gruesome train wreck rendered in beautiful prose as a family splinters into jagged pieces, people's hearts ripped open.

Isaac had decided it was time. It seems that his health and vitality were fading, and who ever knows the day of his death? Although he was generally more quiet and passive throughout his life, he knew it was time to take the initiative and pass the blessing on to his firstborn son. It didn't hurt that Esau was his favorite son, a real man's man...and that tradition dictated that the firstborn be the first in line. Before we get any further in the story, we need to consider what "**the blessing**" really is in this context, and what it represents. It was customary at this time in history and in this part of the world, that the firstborn would inherit the bulk of the family wealth and possessions, with lesser portions given to other siblings. But the blessing that Isaac was ready to confer on his son was the same blessing he had himself received from his father, Abraham, and it involved much more than material possessions. It included the **covenant** that God had made with Abraham and his descendants, the promises of inheriting the land of Canaan, of being God's friend, of being blessed and bringing blessing to the world. It was the favor of God that went with it. It was a mission and a responsibility. It was the most powerful form of affirmation imaginable.

For Esau, the larger aspect of the blessing held no interest; it was too intangible and too far away in the future. He wanted instant gratification here and now. Jacob, however, understood at least something of the value of this blessing, of having a place in this covenant. And to have this kind of affirmation from his father...well, he *had* to have it! He also understood that his father preferred Esau and not him. As much as he wanted it, he knew he didn't have his father's approval and acceptance. He wasn't "bless-able" in his father's view. *If he was going to get anything, he would have to fight or scheme to get it.* So, when his mother came to him saying they had no time to lose, that his father was about to confer the blessing on his older brother, Jacob only argued a little before going along with the plan to deceive Isaac.

I'm going to assume you've read the story by now, how Jacob posed as Esau in order to get the blessing from their father, taking advantage of the old man's near-blindness and his older brother's clothing to pull off this scheme. Let's take another look at the scene. And as we do, imagine for a few moments that you are Jacob...

He went to his father and said, "My father."

"Yes, my son," he answered. "Who is it?"

Jacob said to his father, "I am Esau your firstborn. I have done as you told me. Please sit up and eat some of my game, so that you may give me your blessing."

Isaac asked his son, "How did you find it so quickly, my son?"

"The Lord your God gave me success," he replied.

Then Isaac said to Jacob, "Come near so I can touch you, my son, to know whether you really are my son Esau or not."

Jacob went close to his father Isaac, who touched him and said, "The voice is the voice of Jacob, but the hands are the hands of Esau." He did not recognize him, for his hands were hairy like those of his brother Esau; so he proceeded to bless him.

"Are you really my son Esau?" he asked.

"I am," he replied.

Then he said, "My son, bring me some of your game to eat, so that I may give you my blessing."

Here you are, pretending to be someone else, someone your father can approve of and bless, because you know he'd never accept you for who you really are. If you ever had any hope of that, it's about to be thoroughly crushed.

"Who are you?"

"I'm Esau your firstborn."

"Come here so I can touch you - I want to make sure it's really Esau." (Because that's who I want). And then just to make sure ...

"Are you really my son Esau?"

How are you feeling now? You've just heard it from your father's own mouth who it is that he really prefers (and whom he *doesn't* prefer). Your heart is disintegrating and bleeding out through your pores. If you thought you felt the sting of rejection before, now you're being annihilated by it. But at this point, you might as well go through with the deception and get what you can get...

> Then he [Isaac] said, "My son, bring me some of your game to eat, so that I may give you my blessing."
> Jacob brought it to him and he ate; and he brought some wine and he drank. Then his father Isaac said to him, "Come here, my son, and kiss me."
> So he went to him and kissed him. When Isaac caught the smell of his clothes, he blessed him and said,
> "Ah, the smell of my son is like the smell of a field that the Lord has blessed.
> May God give you heaven's dew and earth's richness— an abundance of grain and new wine.
> May nations serve you and peoples bow down to you.
> Be lord over your brothers, and may the sons of your mother bow down to you.
> May those who curse you be cursed and those who bless you be blessed."

What powerful, beautiful words of affirmation and blessing! Anyone who received words like these would have no self-doubt, no lack of confidence, no questions about their identity and worth in their father's eyes. They would be secure in the present and full of hope for the future—except for Jacob. Even as Jacob managed to wrangle the blessing from his father, he knew these words were not really intended for him, but for his older brother. Rather than healing his wounds and satisfying his craving for approval, rather than filling him with confidence, each pronouncement of blessing must have felt like a hammer-blow of rejection.

It must have taken all his strength to stand there and go through with the deception.

Then, finally, it is done. Jacob has obtained the coveted blessing from his father, Isaac. It would be many years, however, before he was convinced, before he realized and actually accepted that God had chosen him and had decided to bless him from the start. Whatever doubts Jacob still had—and whether or not he realized the truth—his father, Isaac, knew that something real and powerful had transpired during that pronouncement over his son, even if it wasn't the son he had intended to bless! As we see in the story, Jacob had barely left his father (and his discomfort level must have been so high, I'm sure he was in a hurry to get out of there), when Esau came in with the meal he had prepared. There was momentary confusion, and then it all became clear... **Genesis 27:33** says that Isaac "trembled exceedingly, and said, 'Who? Where is the one who hunted game and brought it to me? I ate all of it before you came, and I have blessed him—**and indeed he shall be blessed.**'"

Despite the deception involved, Isaac had evidently felt the prophetic power of the blessing as he had spoken the words over Jacob—it was undeniable. What follows is a scene full of Esau's rage, bitterness, and grief at the turn things have taken. He had assumed that regardless of his choices, attitude, and lifestyle, and in spite of his younger brother's scheming, he had been guaranteed the blessing since he was the firstborn. In his disbelief and rage, there was only one solution he could see: murder. Once again, the boys' mother stepped in to manage things behind the scenes: Jacob was immediately sent to her homeland to find a wife from among their relatives, because, in her words to Isaac, "I am weary of my life because of the daughters of Heth; if Jacob takes a wife of the daughters of Heth (Esau's wives) like these who are the daughters of the land, what good will my life be to me?" Of course, the other reason was that Jacob had to go, or risk being killed by his brother. Rebekah had evidently hidden that piece of information from Isaac.

Her plan was that Jacob's absence would be for "a little while, until your brother's anger subsides, and he forgets what you have done to him." Little did she know that she would never see her favorite son again, and that her firstborn, Esau, though physically present, would be thoroughly estranged. Despite her best efforts at controlling the outcomes, her worst fear was realized: She did lose both of her sons in one day, and she would be long dead before Jacob ever returned home again.

The Twenty-Year Struggle

The next phase of Jacob's life would be marked by intense striving as he wrestled with all his might to overcome obstacles, to get ahead, to prove himself, to outwit the opposition, and to win the material and physical benefits of "the blessing." It would also be a time of learning hard lessons, of being forced to taste his own medicine as he was obliged to deal with someone who was just as skilled at deception, manipulation, and trickery as he himself was!

Jacob's adventure could not have had a more encouraging, auspicious beginning. His father, Isaac, sent him on his way to his mother's relatives with more words of blessing, **and this time the words were spoken deliberately, with full knowledge of who was receiving the blessing**. Isaac had come to realize and accept God's plan for his younger son, and the old man was in full accord. Finally, Jacob had the acceptance and approval from his father that he must have always craved. But would it be enough? On the first night of Jacob's journey, in addition to his father's words of blessing, God gave him a dream and spoke to him directly with powerful words of blessing and affirmation:

> Jacob left Beersheba and set out for Harran. When he reached a certain place, he stopped for the night because the sun had set. Taking one of the stones there, he put it under his head and lay down to sleep. He had a dream in which he saw a stairway resting on the earth, with its top reaching to heaven, and the angels of God were ascending and descending on it. There above it stood the Lord, and he said: "I am the Lord, the God of your father Abraham and the God of Isaac. I will give you and your descendants the land on which you are lying. Your descendants will be like the dust of the earth, and you will spread out to the west and to the east, to the north and to the south. All peoples on earth will be blessed through you and your offspring. I am with you and will watch over you wherever you go, and I will bring you back to this land. I will not leave you until I have done what I have promised you" (Genesis 28:10–16).

Wow! God Himself appeared and spoke to Jacob in a dream at the outset of his journey, assuring him that he was chosen to inherit the blessing, that the Lord was intimately, actively involved in his life (as the angels were busily coming and going between heaven and earth), and that He would be with him all the way. That should have been enough to convince anyone! But Jacob was not yet convinced. He had heard, but not really received, the words of blessing from both his earthly father and from God Himself.

When your life has been shaped by rejection, when you've been the one not chosen, not preferred, year after year, it drives a lie deep into your heart and mind: "I am not acceptable, I am not the one God wants, I'm not the one people will want. I am not enough. I will have to work extra hard to gain acceptance, approval, and anything else in life that is good." Some people who struggle with rejection and identity issues choose not to engage in the struggle—they simply withdraw and live on the fringes of life as timid observers. Others, like Jacob, will fight tooth and nail to prove themselves. But until you receive the blessing, and your true name along with it, no amount of struggle or achievement will ever be enough.

Note Jacob's response to what God told him in this dream. He was in awe, because, in his words, "The Lord is in this place, and I did not know it!" He set up a monument and named the place Bethel—which means "the house of God." But even his awe of God's presence was not enough to convince his heart concerning his true identity, as one who was chosen for blessing. He made a vow that was predicated on a giant "IF."

> Early the next morning Jacob took the stone he had placed under his head and set it up as a pillar and poured oil on top of it. He called that place Bethel, though the city used to be called Luz. Then Jacob made a vow, saying, "**If** God will be with me and will watch over me on this journey I am taking and will give me food to eat and clothes to wear so that I return safely to my father's household, **then** the Lord will be my God and this stone that I have set up as a pillar will be God's house, and of all that you give me I will give you a tenth." (Gen. 28:18-22).

All of this sounds great, but do you see Jacob's approach here? Even though God had clearly spoken about the blessing and told Jacob what He would do, in Jacob's mind it still remained to be seen. I don't think he was doubting God's ability to keep His word; he was doubting his own worthiness and acceptability to receive it. His struggle with identity—with seeing himself as someone whom God had chosen—was far from settled. Between the "if" and the "then" of Jacob's vow would be twenty long years of struggle, during which God's mercies were both kind and severe. Kind, in that during this time the Lord mercifully blessed Jacob with a growing family, abundant provision, and protection. Severe, in that God placed Jacob in direct relationship and conflict with someone who was very much like himself—determined, skilled at deception, and used to having his own way. In this relationship with his uncle Laban, Jacob would repeatedly reap what he had sown. God's merciful purpose in these circumstances was to bring Jacob the schemer to the end of himself, to the end of his stubborn striving, and to bring him into the freedom of surrender to the One who had chosen him for blessing. (If you still haven't done so, now would be a good time to read Genesis 29 through 31.)

Surrender to Win

I appreciate Alcoholics Anonymous for their thorough, step-by-step approach to conquering addiction through biblical principles, which are distilled into twelve very practical steps. The first three steps could be summed up like this: "My attempts to control and manage life on my own have failed—I cannot do it on my own. I believe there is a God who is good and who has the power to restore me, so I've made a conscious choice to surrender/submit my life to His care and direction." The remaining nine steps spell out in very practical terms what this surrender looks like in daily life and how to walk it out. Over the years, AA folks have come up with a number of pithy sayings that sum up these principles and make them easy to remember. One of my favorites is "surrender to win." This is not just good advice for those with a chemical addiction. It's an inexorable principle of relationship with the Father, since none of us can save ourselves—but we sure like to try!

For Jacob, it would take a crisis completely beyond his ability to manage before he would surrender. It would take being faced with the potential loss of everything he had worked for and everyone he loved to bring him to this place of letting go of control, admitting his helplessness, and clinging instead to the God who wanted only to bless him. In the end, **it would be through surrender that he would overcome and receive his new name...**

Things started out well enough for Jacob as he began to work for his uncle Laban. Not only did he find a suitable candidate for a wife, but he fell deeply in love with Laban's younger daughter, Rachel. Unwittingly, he also fell into a rivalry between Rachel and her firstborn sister, Leah. Jacob had been so desperate to have the rights of the firstborn, but those rights were about to be served up to him in a way he had never anticipated... After working for Laban for seven years, it was time for the wedding, and Jacob could hardly contain his excitement to finally have and hold his beloved Rachel. It wasn't until the next morning—his bride having been appropriately veiled until reaching the darkness of the wedding tent—that he realized the truth. The bride in his bed was Leah, *the firstborn*, disguised as the second-born Rachel! He was understandably outraged and stomped off to confront Laban, who calmly explained (with a shrewd smile, no doubt) that it just wasn't done, to give the younger in marriage before the older. *The rights of the firstborn had to be respected!*

The years of hard lessons had begun—years during which Jacob's own self-serving behavior would be mirrored back to him, within a circle of familial relationships from which he could not run. And the conflict was not limited to the battle of wits and wills between him and his uncle. There was the bitter rivalry in his own household between his two wives, Rachel and Leah, and he was forced to witness firsthand the pain and sadness of the one who was not chosen, and the shame of the other, who could not attain to the blessing of bearing children. He would learn to see things from another perspective as he witnessed his own desperate striving to get ahead and prove himself played out in the lives of these two women. It seemed that everything in his life had become a mirror, and the reflection was not pleasant. Mercy is not always a gentle thing when we are stubborn like Jacob, because God's determination to bless us is always stronger than our determination to have our own way.

Throughout all the family drama and bad behavior, God was still at work bringing the promised blessing to pass. The family grew, the flocks and herds increased, and Jacob became more and more successful. But he seemed to think it was all due to his own feverish efforts to outwit his uncle and gain the upper hand. Laban changed the terms of their agreement ten times. Rachel and Leah continued to vie for their husband's attention. Life became one epic wrestling match, and Jacob could never relax, never loosen his grip for a moment. He was too busy trying to stay one step ahead of disaster to be able to perceive God's invitation to surrender and receive the blessing; he would continue to fight instead. Maybe that sounds familiar?

Finally, things reached a tipping point. It became evident that any goodwill that had ever existed between Jacob and his uncle had evaporated in the heat of their vendetta, a vendetta that had never been openly acknowledged. Jacob heard that Laban's sons were more or less accusing him of stealing their father's wealth in order to build up his own. Jacob also realized that the thin veneer of civility, which had until now kept all the mistrust and resentments under the surface, had finally worn through. It didn't feel safe anymore. In the midst of these circumstances, God spoke to Jacob that it was time to go home. He had a meeting with Rachel and Leah, who were in full agreement, confessing that they felt like strangers in their father's house and that they were more than ready to leave. In this candid family conversation, we hear Jacob acknowledge for the first time that his success and wealth had been a result of the Lord's faithfulness and providence toward him and his family, and not simply the fruit of his own striving to get the upper hand. He was finally beginning to understand that God really did intend to bless him, but fear was still very much in the driver's seat and Jacob was still the schemer, determined to run his own show and to selfishly manipulate events—which is why he deceived his uncle and fled secretly with his wives, children, servants, workers, and droves of livestock, while Laban was away. This is an amazing feat that had to have taken more than a little planning, and I think it reveals something of the degree of anxiety and desperation that drove Jacob on any given day. But the worst—or best—was yet to come...

In Psalm 139:5, the psalmist says to the Lord, "You hem me in behind and before, and you lay your hand upon me." For the writer of the psalm, this was a comforting thought, but to someone like Jacob who must always be in control, this is terrifying! When we are like Jacob, struggling to prove ourselves, striving to get ahead, and not convinced about God's good intentions for us, we can never rest. The Lord will let us run ourselves ragged in our attempts to manage everything—up to a point. And then He just might arrange circumstances, like a dragnet that is drawn progressively tighter, so that we are "hemmed in" and can run no more—because eventually we need to face our fears, face the past, face ourselves, and ultimately face God. This is exactly what happened to Jacob.

A New Name

Laban pursued Jacob and eventually caught up with him. It was a tense confrontation, but they were able to part on peaceful terms. This is because God had already intervened and told Laban in a dream to "stand down" and not interfere with His plans for Jacob. The Lord had His own plans, and there was a much more serious confrontation awaiting Jacob just up ahead...

Just as on the outbound journey twenty years before, when Jacob had been given the reassurance of God's accompanying presence and activity in his life, so on the return journey, he was met by the "angels of God" (Genesis 32:1–2). I'm not even going to speculate on the details, because none are given. I think the point is that once again, Jacob was given a supernatural encounter as an assurance that he was not alone. There were "two camps," as the name he gave this place (*mahanaim*) indicates—his entourage and the Lord's camp somewhere nearby. He was going to need that reassurance! (And for you, the reader, be assured that a loving Father is involved, very near, and actively at work to do you good, however things may appear at the moment.)

Jacob's brother, Esau, had evidently become quite prosperous, and so powerful that he controlled an entire territory, which Jacob and his group must pass through on the way home. Always a man with a plan, Jacob prepared a lavish gift of flocks and herds for his brother (maybe an attempt at restitution?), and he sent servants ahead to deliver it, along with a humble, conciliatory message from "your servant, Jacob." To properly move into the future, he had to deal with the unresolved issues of his past— there was no detour available. And that is as true for each of us as it was for Jacob, which is the reason we're looking at his story in such detail here.

Jacob's servants returned to camp with some terrifying news: Esau himself was coming to meet his brother, along with four hundred armed men. It seems that he hadn't forgotten what his scheming brother had done to him, and for Jacob, twenty years' worth of unresolved guilt had magnified his fear until it was now palpable. He planned, he prayed, and he did both with desperation. He was humbly crying out to God and acknowledging that everything he had was a result of the Lord's blessing, but he was also anticipating the worst and making contingency plans. As always, he was doing his utmost to control the situation and manipulate the outcome.

> In great fear and distress Jacob divided the people who were with him into two groups, and the flocks and herds and camels as well. He thought, "If Esau comes and attacks one group, the group that is left may escape" (Gen. 32:7–8).

He then sent an entire parade of servants with more gifts of livestock to his brother, Esau, hoping to appease him. In the night, he escorted his immediate family and his most precious possessions across a stream that had to be forded, planning then to go on ahead of them all to face his brother. So far, his detailed plan was being executed flawlessly—and then the unexpected happens...

> That night Jacob got up and took his two wives, his two female servants and his eleven sons and crossed the ford of the Jabbok. After he had sent them across the stream, he sent over all his possessions. So Jacob was left alone, and a man wrestled with him till daybreak. When the man saw that he could not overpower him, he touched the socket of Jacob's hip so that his hip was wrenched as he wrestled with the man" (Gen 32:22–25).

At the most critical moment, just as Jacob had gotten every last detail in place and every last person where he wanted them to be, and just as he was about to go on ahead of his family to oversee everything, he was stopped in his tracks. Take note of how the story is told. The Scripture says: "A Man wrestled with him until the breaking of the day." Jacob was not the aggressor here, and he sure didn't have time for a friendly wrestling match with a stranger! Everything he owned and all of his people—essentially his entire life—was across the stream, Esau was on his way, and there was not a moment to lose! He must have been wild with panic, and he wrestled with all his might to break free from this divine opponent. He couldn't seem to break loose, but he couldn't stop trying, either: Such was the measure of his stubborn determination to stay in control, and such was the depth of his fear. Finally, this "Man" (who was really the Lord in human form) abruptly ended the wrestling match by putting Jacob's hip out of joint, rendering him nearly helpless. Maybe it was at this point of momentary shock and helplessness that Jacob realized whom he had been struggling against, and now instead of fighting against Him, he was clinging to Him. The moment of full surrender was near as his deep need for the Lord and his own inability to fix everything became crystal clear.

The Man calmly said, "Okay, I need to get going. It's daybreak." If Jacob had been panicked before, the thought of being left in this condition with no help forthcoming was even more terrifying.

> But Jacob replied, "I will not let you go unless you bless me."
> The man asked him, "What is your name?"
> "Jacob," he answered. (Gen. 32:26–27).

The moment of truth had come. No more conniving and scheming to get the blessing. No more disguises as he came face-to-face with the One who knew him to the core. This time he must come as he really is, humble himself, and ask openly: "Bless me!" He must also answer the identity question and take responsibility for who he has been all these years: Jacob, the deceiver. Will it mean rejection? Refusal? No, it will mean a release into his true identity.

> "Then the man said, "Your name will no longer be Jacob, but Israel, because you have struggled with God and with humans and have overcome" (Gen. 32:28).

The real struggle for Jacob was to arrive at this place of surrender—surrender to the only One who could give him his true name. Remember? Surrender to win. His parents gave him the name Jacob, but God gave him his true name, Israel: prince of God.

> Jacob said, "Please tell me your name."
> But he replied, "Why do you ask my name?" Then he blessed him there. (Gen. 32:29).

Did you get that? He blessed him **there**. Where? In that place of surrender and face-to-face encounter. God wrestled Jacob to the ground not to punish him, *but to bless him*. The thing Jacob had struggled for, deceived and connived and slaved and fought for, that he had disguised himself to get—because he could never believe he was actually chosen, could never believe he would be accepted for who he was, could never believe he was good enough for—he finally received it in this place where all the striving stops and humble dependence begins.

"So Jacob called the place Peniel, saying, "It is because I saw God face to face, and yet my life was spared." The sun rose above him as he passed Peniel, and he was limping because of his hip" (Gen. 32:30–31). He was limping, but he was limping into daybreak.

Many of us have struggled like Jacob to prove ourselves, to get ahead, to win approval and get the blessing, never really convinced that we are acceptable, that we are "bless-able." Maybe the important authority figures in your life didn't give you "the blessing," the approval and the affirmation we all crave. Maybe you've twisted yourself into various shapes over the years to be the person that you think others will like. Maybe you've lived under the stress of constant, feverish effort to control your world, believing you are on your own and that it will all fall apart if you ever loosen your grip. Learn from Jacob and surrender earlier rather than later. You are the one the Father has chosen to bless, and no disguises are necessary. Stop running, face Him, and receive your true name. It will be the start of a new day.

8

The Conflict between Divine Revelation and Human Reason

"This is the covenant I will establish with the people of Israel after that time, declares the Lord.
I will put my laws in their minds and write them on their hearts.
I will be their God, and they will be my people.
No longer will they teach their neighbor, or say to one another, 'Know the Lord,'
because they will all know me, from the least of them to the greatest.
For I will forgive their wickedness and will remember their sins no more." (Hebrews 8:10-12)

Those who live according to the flesh have their minds set on what the flesh desires; but those who live in accordance with the Spirit have their minds set on what the Spirit desires. The mind governed by the flesh is death, but the mind governed by the Spirit is life and peace. (Rom. 8:5-6)

The human mind is incredibly complex and capable of so many amazing things!

During our first three and half years in Congo, our two older boys, Matt and Jamie, had both picked up the local language with the ease that children do. Back in the States for a furlough year, I would often try to speak Lingala with the boys in an effort to keep up our language skills. Jamie had no trouble understanding my Lingala when I spoke to him, but he would always answer me in English. It seemed that now that we were back in America, he didn't want to use his second language, so I asked him about it. He explained it to me this way:

"Dad, when we're in America, Lingala moves to the back of my brain and English moves to the front. Then when we're back in Congo, Lingala will come around to the front of my brain and English will move to the back." (He demonstrated the smoothness of this cerebral maneuver with his hands, one on his forehead and the other at the back of his head, then sliding them around to the reverse.) I'm not sure how scientific that explanation was, but I certainly got his point!

Scientists are still delving into the mysteries of how the human mind works, how it interacts with the body, with our environment, and with others in our networks of human relationships. Our mind's ability to reason, to analyze, to make decisions, to use existing data to envision what the future may hold, or to envision solutions to current problems—as well as all the emotions that are intertwined with these processes of our minds—all of this is a reflection of our Creator God, who made us in His image.

Our minds are incredibly powerful, but that power can be both a blessing and a curse! Have you ever been sabotaged by worry or crippled by indecision, as your mind keeps offering up one scenario after another of what might happen, what could go wrong, or continually balancing out the pros and cons of a course of action in an endless loop until you want to scream? What about those rationalizations your mind cooks up when you want to justify doing something that you know is wrong? That powerful brain of yours becomes your partner in crime, doesn't it? The point I'm making is this: In spite of how powerful and amazing the human mind is, it is definitely **not** infallible, and no matter how foolproof our logic may seem at times, it might just be entirely wrong!

Two Trees and Some Very Bad Logic

Once again, to get a true perspective on the value and limits of human reasoning, we need to go back to the beginning and take another look at God's original plan. As was pointed out in chapter 3 of this book, "Hearing the Father's Voice," we saw in the first two chapters of Genesis that Adam and Eve lived by **divine revelation**. Simply put, whatever they knew, they knew it because God told them about it. He explained and interpreted life to them. In those original words of blessing (Genesis 1:26–28), God explained to our first parents who they were, what life was about, and what His purpose was for them and for the world. It is clear they would need to employ their powerful minds—as yet undimmed by sin and rebellion—to partner with God in developing the world and bringing it under His rule. **But human reasoning was empowered and guided by divine revelation.** Man was living by "every word that comes from the mouth of God." It was life to listen to the Father.

From the moment when Adam and Eve chose the serpent's lies over God's revealed truth, their ability to properly reason was corrupted. **In choosing to eat from the Tree of Knowledge—as opposed to sticking with the Tree of Life—they were choosing**

to live by fallible human reasoning instead of by divine revelation, and it has been that way ever since. Whenever people are disconnected from the Father and His words, reasoning becomes king, and it doesn't always steer us in the right direction—whether it's based on the fallacies of ancient superstitions or on the facts of modern science. Lest someone misunderstand, I am not devaluing science here! I'm truly thankful for modern science and the countless ways the discoveries of dedicated scientists have improved our lives, from agriculture to zoology and all the things in between—including modern medicine and mechanics. Good science is actually the practice of God's original command to develop and rule the earth; it's not an enemy of faith! However, we must be aware that even indisputable facts can result in bad conclusions, *not because the facts are faulty, but because our reasoning is so easily corrupted by any number of things*—especially the desire to be our own god and to do our own thing.

Choosing between the Tree of Life and the Tree of Knowledge

When someone makes the choice to follow Jesus and to be restored to relationship with the Father, a process begins, which the New Testament calls the "renewing of the mind" (Romans 12:2) or "being made new in the attitude of your mind" (Ephesians 4:23). In several of his letters to various churches, the apostle Paul outlined the stark difference between "the mind that is governed by the flesh" and the mind "governed by the Spirit," between those who live "in the futility of their thinking, separated from the life of God," and those who are "being made new in the attitude of their minds" according to the truth. But this is definitely a **process that requires our ongoing participation**, not an instantaneous event!

From the moment this renewing process begins, there is a tug-of-war between our native tendency to make human reasoning king, and the call to obey the truth as it has been given to us in Christ. Will we live, choose, and make decisions according to the dictates of our own fallible logic, which is so easily influenced by a multitude of factors (like family, culture, selfish desires, fears, etc.), or will we choose to live by divine revelation? Will we feed ourselves from the Tree of Knowledge, or will we feed from the Tree of Life? It seems like a simple choice, a "no-brainer" as we like to say, but in real life the lines are so often blurred and the struggle becomes very real. There is an exchange between the disciple Peter and Jesus, in Matthew 16, that illustrates this struggle so clearly. I feel like I should apologize to Peter for picking on him yet again, but it's all there for us in the gospel accounts, and I didn't write them—I'm just hoping to learn from them! Let's have a look:

> When Jesus came to the region of Caesarea Philippi, he asked his disciples, "Who do people say the Son of Man is?"
>
> They replied, "Some say John the Baptist; others say Elijah; and still others, Jeremiah or one of the prophets."
>
> "But what about you?" he asked. "Who do you say I am?"
>
> Simon Peter answered, "You are the Messiah, the Son of the living God."
>
> Jesus replied, "Blessed are you, Simon son of Jonah, for this was not revealed to you by flesh and blood, but by my Father in heaven. And I tell you that you are Peter, and on this rock I will build my church, and the gates of Hades will not overcome it. I will give you the keys of the kingdom of heaven; whatever you bind on earth will be bound in heaven, and whatever you loose on earth will be loosed in heaven." Then he ordered his disciples not to tell anyone that he was the Messiah.

> From that time on Jesus began to explain to his disciples that he must go to Jerusalem and suffer many things at the hands of the elders, the chief priests and the teachers of the law, and that he must be killed and on the third day be raised to life.
>
> Peter took him aside and began to rebuke him. "Never, Lord!" he said. "This shall never happen to you!"
>
> Jesus turned and said to Peter, "Get behind me, Satan! You are a stumbling block to me; you do not have in mind the concerns of God, but merely human concerns." (Matt. 16:13-23)

In the short space of ten verses, Peter hit one of the highest points in his journey as a disciple of Jesus—and one of the lowest. Jesus had just popped the big question to his disciples, "Who do you say I am? You've given Me others' opinions, but what about you?" Peter landed on the truth and declared, "You are the Christ, the Son of the living God." Jesus congratulated him, because this was not merely a conclusion reached by human reasoning. If human reasoning were enough, all of Jesus' miracles should have led everyone to that same conclusion. But because of our brokenness, our stubbornness, and our sinfulness, we need more than that. We need revelation. And this is exactly what Peter had received—divine revelation. It was not flesh and blood, Jesus said, but His Father in heaven who had enabled Peter to see this!

Imagine yourself in Peter's place, having this conversation with Jesus. You are feeling really, really good at this moment. Maybe the others don't really get it, but you do! You are in the know, you are totally sure about which way this train is headed—and you're on it. *Thrones and kingdoms, here we come!* As a matter of fact, you are now so sure of your ability to see the big picture that you see yourself as ready to be in the driver's seat. You're even more sure of the right direction than Jesus Himself is...which is why you have to step in and stop this crazy talk. Suffering, rejection, crucifixion? *Jesus, what are You talking about? C'mon, Lord, You're going to discourage the troops with that kind of negativity. This will never happen to You!*

Suddenly, Jesus turned quick as lightning and was up in Peter's face with the harshest rebuke any of them have ever heard:

"Get behind me Satan! You are a stumbling block to me; you do not have in mind the concerns of God, but merely human concerns."

I wonder if tears sprang to Peter's eyes. Or was he momentarily too shocked to react at all? If this had been me, I know I would have been hurt and angry at first, and I would have felt truly humiliated standing there with all the other disciples looking on. How could Peter have been so right one moment, but so wrong the next? Human reasoning and logic had taken over: *Jesus is the Messiah, the Son of God! A proper Messiah doesn't get rejected and crucified; He conquers, He overcomes, and He ascends to a throne...*

The Way Back

God's plan to rescue us from sin, Satan, and death was not obvious to Peter, and it wouldn't have been obvious to us, either, if we had been in his place. It was so contrary to common human reasoning, that the apostle Paul said that to the Greeks, who revered wisdom, the Cross was actual foolishness. To the Jews, it was an offense to their cherished religious ideas. Those of us today have the benefit of looking back, knowing how it all turned out, so it's easy for us to shake our heads at Peter's assumptions and misinformed actions. We need to be careful, however, because it's still deceptively simple for us to make assumptions about how things should go and what God's plan should look like. When

God shows me something, I get excited about the possibilities (about how this is going to make me look so good, or advance my career, etc.), and I'm off and running. "Thanks, Lord, I'll take it from here!" Nobody can reason with me now, because *God told me*. That trumps everything. Who knows how many times sincere, enthusiastic Christians have ended up confused, disillusioned, and even angry when their vision didn't pan out the way they just knew it would. There is safety in remaining humble and teachable, because we never know it all and because His ways really are higher than ours!

But back to Jesus and Peter. Why was this rebuke so harsh? Because Jesus was opening the way back to the Father through humble obedience, by doing the exact opposite of what Adam and Eve had done in the garden. Rather than living according to human reasoning, which doubts God's wisdom and justice, and which would tempt Him to avoid the cross, Jesus was choosing to live by revelation, "by every word that comes from the mouth of God." Instead of choosing the Tree of Knowledge, Jesus was choosing a different tree—the Cross. This ultimate obedience and humble submission to the Father's will—the Cross—has now become for us the Tree of Life. Jesus rebuked Peter so harshly because the only way back to the Father, trust and obedience, which teaches us to live by divine revelation rather than by human reason, was being challenged. Jesus had to expose this challenge for what it was—flawed, human reasoning based not on pure motives, but on the idea of self-advancement and self-preservation. It was reasoning cut from the same cloth as Satan's temptation of Jesus in the wilderness, and his temptation of Adam and Eve in the Garden of Eden at the dawn of time.

It's All about Trust

If we are going to grow in our relationship with the Father, we need to submit our reasoning—whether in decision-making, future-planning, relationship-building, or finances—to the light of God's Word. But *why* is this such a struggle at times? After all, none of us would insist that we know everything or that our reasoning and logic is infallible. So, why do we consistently seek to make our imperfect human reasoning king and give it the final word? The very idea of *submitting* to a direction or a process, of obeying when we don't fully understand—it's uncomfortable to say the least, and for some of us, downright terrifying.

I believe that for most of us, it comes down to a trust issue. Our first parents began life in the context of an intimate relationship with the Father, and their knowledge of God was a personal, **relational** knowledge, based on trust in Him, versus a rational knowledge of mere facts learned *about* Him. In this relationship of trust, they didn't have to know every detail about everything before obeying. They simply trusted what God had said because they already knew His character, His perfect goodness, and His love. There was safety in this relationship, and it was this child-like trust that Satan belittled and attacked. He still attacks it today, at every opportunity—from the time when we are little children who are so ready to trust and believe what we are told. In this fallen world, promises are broken, and disappointment ensues. Or worse, maybe the very people you trusted to protect and care for you did the exact opposite and neglected or abused you. You learned that life is not safe, and that trust is not an option. Your true Father is supremely trustworthy and will never, ever do you harm—only good. You know this on an intellectual level, but fear may still claw at your soul as you attempt to surrender and trust Him. He understands, and He will meet you more than halfway.

In choosing to eat from the Tree of the Knowledge of Good and Evil, Adam and Eve exchanged their personal, relational knowledge of God for a knowledge that would enable them to be their own gods—or so they were told. They would know as much as God Himself knew (a ridiculous lie!), and thus be free to make up their own minds about what was good and what was evil, and control their own destiny. To live from the Tree of Knowledge means that, instead of being directed by a relationship with the Father based on trust and obedience, I'm going to reason everything out for myself and live according to what I think—or maybe by what the crowd thinks, or what my peers believe, or what my culture or political party dictates.

Sadly, many "believers" live like this every day. Theoretically, they are believers, but in practice they are functional atheists living on their own in the world. I will be completely honest here and say that I'm not that brave. The thought of being on my own in this world is terrifying! It's not that I don't struggle with obedience at times, but once you begin to know the Father, you'll find that childlike trust is so much less stressful than running your own show!

In our broken world full of broken promises, it may feel right and natural to trust yourself and to rely on your own reasoning. It feels good to be in control, doesn't it? This is a huge blind spot for many of us—that we are more comfortable trusting our own minds than we are trusting God's infallible wisdom! I have let myself down often enough that I am learning—however wise I might think I am—to submit my reasoning on any issue to the scrutiny of God's Word. **Proverbs 3:5–8** says it like this:

> Trust in the Lord with all your heart and lean not on
> your own understanding;

In all your ways submit to him, and he will make your
paths straight.
Do not be wise in your own eyes; fear the Lord and
shun evil.
This will bring health to your body and nourishment
to your bones.

And **Romans 16:19–20** says it this way:

> Everyone has heard about your obedience, so I rejoice
> because of you; **but I want you to be wise about what
> is good, and innocent about what is evil.** The God of
> peace will soon crush Satan under your feet.

The more our thinking is informed and shaped by God's revelation in Christ and grounded in His Word, the deeper our
fellowship with the Father will become. The more we choose
trust over control, the more victory we will experience! These
verses in Romans 16 are a direct reference to what happened
in Genesis 3, when Adam and Eve ate from the wrong tree. As
our Representative and Champion, Jesus reversed that deadly
decision for the human race, and blazed a trail back to the Tree
of Life by His humble obedience and trust, choosing to live by
revelation rather than by human reasoning. Now it's our turn to
follow Him on that path back to an intimate, trusting relationship
with the Father.

9

The Need for Emotional Restoration

"Stop crying or I'll give you something to cry about!"

That's a common parental threat that many of us heard at one time or another during our childhood years, and it was probably warranted on occasion! (Not that I think careless threats shouted in frustration are a healthy way to deal with a pouting or disobedient child, but most of us learned in our early years how to manipulate the adults in our lives through tears or tantrums, and it's a mercy if someone was there to call our bluff rather than give in to those manipulations.)

In my years of pastoral counseling, however, I've heard more than one story of an angry or overwhelmed parent forbidding their child to cry when the family dog died ("It's just an animal!"), their best friend moved away, or some other pain or loss was experienced. And underneath the callous words, the real reason, if the parent could have verbalized it, was simply this: "I don't have the patience or the resources or the know-how to comfort you right now, and your tears are going to push me over the edge—so you need to stop!"

I've heard even worse, too: children who were forbidden to cry or grieve at the death of a parent, or even to talk about the loss or the missing member of the family.

It's no secret that in many families, people are uncomfortable with emotions in general, and they don't really know how to express their own, or respond to others', feelings. No one really talks about what is going on in their hearts. After all, emotions are inconvenient, embarrassing things, like a sudden rip in the seat of your pants or some other wardrobe malfunction that threatens to leave you exposed in front of everyone. No, we would rather get out of sight and put things back together as quickly as possible! *Hopefully nobody noticed...*

Then there is the other extreme, those families in which the emotional climate is volatile and stormy. Outbursts of anger, rage, or tears are common, unpredictable moods are constantly on display, and there is the underlying assumption that "I can't help how I feel!"—especially when those feelings are being conveniently dumped on the nearest available victim. Experience has taught some of us that emotions are simply dangerous, uncharted waters that are best left unexplored—there be monsters down there!

The flipside of the inability to express, understand, and deal with "negative" emotions like grief, anger, or shame is the inability to express unbridled joy or excitement, to fully experience delight, and even to express love as it should be expressed. For many, even these positive feelings are cause for embarrassment and discomfort if they are expressed too freely. The big question is "Why?" Why are so many of us stunted or seemingly handi-capped when it comes to this facet of our humanity?

A God-Breathed Facet of Our Humanity

Once again, it's instructive to go back to the beginning, to have another look at the original condition of humanity in the Garden, to consider again God's original purpose for the human race and that untainted relationship Adam and Eve had with God and with one another before it was broken. Then we need to look again at the tragic consequences that ensued when they rejected that relationship, in Genesis 3.

We know that man was designed in the image of God. When God the Father breathed into the man's nostrils the breath of life and man became a living being, he was endowed not only with intellect and free will, but also with the capacity to experience a full range of emotions. He was fully functional and able to relate to and experience God—as well as the world around him—on an intellectual, volitional, *and* emotional level. These three aspects, which I believe the Bible is referring to when it speaks of the "heart" of man, were intended to work together in synergy, directed by divine revelation, as man grew in relationship and partnership with God.

Although it is not explicitly stated in these first three chapters of Genesis, I think it is implicit that the original environment—the emotional climate, we could say—of the Garden was **love**. The original pronouncement on everything God had created, and to-ward the manner in which He created it, was this: "And it was good. And it was very good!" Then we see the more intimate details of the creation of mankind in chapter 2—God the Father's very personal touch in forming man, His concern for our joy and satisfaction in providing "every tree that was a delight to the eye and good for food," and His loving concern that we not be alone. This was a world of beauty, order, and abundance in which life could be lived in the glory of relationship and partnership with a good God, a God who loves His children and wants only good things for them. There was nothing to fear and no reason to hide. In the New Testament, the apostle John tells us that "God is love" (1 John 4:8). Love is intrinsic to God's nature and character, so it is much more than an emotion, but it was certainly the *foundation* for our first parents' experience of emotion. Love is that safe and secure relational environment in which we were all meant to grow into maturity—maturity in our experience and expression of emotions, as well as in the exercise of our intellect and will. It was the environment in which Adam and Eve lived.

The Damaging, Deadening Effects of Sin

When our first parents chose independence from God in place of intimacy with Him and severed that relationship, the loss was incalculable. God had warned them that on the day they ate of the Tree of Knowledge, they would die. It's clear that they didn't die physically on that day, but death came to their spirits, and a radical change took place in their ability to experience and respond to the presence of God. Every aspect of their lives was then affected by their disobedience—and the entire created order was affected, as well—but one very immediate impact was **the emotional impact that is with us still to this day.**

> Then the man and his wife heard the sound of the Lord God as he was walking in the garden in the cool of the day, and they hid from the Lord God among the trees of the garden. But the Lord God called to the man, "Where are you?"
> He answered, "I heard you in the garden, and I was afraid because I was naked; so I hid" (Gen. 3:8–10).

It is unspeakably sad that **fear** is the first emotion explicitly mentioned in the Bible. Before this tragic event took place, I am sure that Adam and Eve delighted to walk and talk with Father God in the Garden. I am sure they drew comfort and joy from His nearness, more than any human child has ever experienced in the arms of his or her daddy. But now, the same presence that used to bring joy only struck fear into their hearts. What used to bring comfort and security now felt like a menace. The sad reality is that *fear replaced love as the primary emotion experienced by human beings. When fear is the driving force in one's life, then self-protection becomes the primary motivation—and it has been that way ever since.* **Here is another reason why relationships are so hard: Our need for connection and our reflex of self-protection are in constant tension with one another.**

Guess what emotion is next mentioned by name in the Bible? We don't have to go very far to find it: *anger*, in Genesis 4, and it leads to the first murder. Fear is like cursed ground, poisoned soil that perverts and stunts our emotional development. The two things it produces best are sadness and anger, and right here is the emotional story of the human race. It is the story of one family after another: Mom is sad, and Dad is angry. I am making a huge generalization here, I know, but I make it simply because this is the story I've heard over and over. In so many cultures, anger is perhaps the only "acceptable" emotion for a man to show, because it looks so much like power (even though it is often the very lack of power and the inability to control something that makes a man so angry).

The fact is, anytime we turn away from God and His truth, anytime we seek our own satisfaction or salvation in anything less than Him, we lose some piece of our humanity, and some facet of our God-given faculties and sensibilities is deadened, because sin brings death. The Bible calls it a "hardening of the heart." For many of us, through the ups and downs of life and because of sinful choices—both ours and others'—our emotions have been deadened. We've constructed walls of self-protection against feeling too much of anything. For others, their emotions are disordered, and their emotional reactions are out of proportion to the thing that first brought on those reactions. Peace seems impossible to find. Some people seem to have virtually no emotional response to life, and, on the opposite extreme, some are a heaving mass of volatile emotions ready to spill over at any moment. Sometimes the same person can swing back and forth between these two extremes! But there is good news. God has a restoration plan that includes the entirety of our personhood. Hebrews 7:25 says that Jesus "is able to save completely those who come to God through him, because he always lives to intercede for them." That includes healing for the emotional aspect of our being.

Behold the Man

In Jesus, who is our Example as well as our Savior, we see a man fully alive, in intimate relationship with God the Father, led and empowered by the Holy Spirit. His emotions were as fully functional as His intellect and His will, and He related to heaven and earth with all three aspects engaged and active. Here are a few examples from His life to consider:

> And a leper came to Jesus, beseeching Him and falling on his knees before Him, and saying, "If You are willing, You can make me clean." **Moved with compassion**, Jesus stretched out His hand and touched him, and said to him, "I am willing; be cleansed." Immediately the leprosy left him and he was cleansed. (Mark 1:40–42).

It was not only Jesus' intellect and will that were involved here: *Hmmm. I see that this man needs healing... The Father has sent Me to heal... I'm going to heal this leper... Be healed!* Jesus was not cold and clinical in His approach. His emotions were as fully involved in the situation as were His mind and His will, and they helped to direct His actions! These things worked together as He was moved with compassion, so that God's will would be done and His goodness was displayed in a way that was both powerful *and* relational. We can see Jesus' emotional involvement with needy, suffering people throughout the gospels. Without healthy emotional engagement, we, too, will not be able to do God's will fully and effectively, since God's plan is to partner with us to bring about His will on earth as it is in heaven, and to do it by working through our restored humanity.

At other times, we see Jesus full of joy (Luke 10:21), or sighing deeply with frustration or sadness (Mark 8:12), or consumed with zeal or a holy outrage (John 2:15–17), or even openly weeping (John 11:33–35). These things were not veiled, and there was no shame in them, because they were healthy emotional responses to the situations the Lord was experiencing in those moments. The fact that these emotional responses were observed, remembered, and especially remarked on by Jesus' disciples and others, and ultimately recorded in the gospel accounts, should tell us something about their importance. Here is the True Man, the One and Only sent from the Father, and His glory was being witnessed. Here is man (true humanity) as he was always meant to be. The ability to feel, to feel what we ought to feel to the degree that we should feel it, is a mark of wholeness and freedom. Most importantly, however, is that the Father wants to meet us and to make Himself known to us on the level of our emotions, as well as through the intellect and the will. There are aspects of God that we cannot experience or grasp apart from healthy emotional engagement.

The Path to Restoration

It's one thing to agree that the emotional aspect of our being is God-breathed and a vital part of our being, as we are made in His image, but to experience a renewal or restoration in this realm—that is where many of us feel lost. It may seem like we're dealing with a hopelessly tangled ball of string: Where to begin to sort it out, and how? Or we may wonder whether it's even necessary. In some streams of Christian teaching, emotions have been minimized and deemed irrelevant, while intellect has been set on the throne. After all, the validity of our faith in Christ is based on facts and is not dependent on how we may feel from day to day; it's what we know that counts. While this is true, our emotions certainly affect how we perceive truth, how we relate to God and to those around us, and how well we function and walk in the truth. God wants us to be whole and fully functional in every aspect of our being.

We must remember that God is **Spirit** (John 4:24), not cold intellect. God is **Spirit**, not an impersonal will. He is not a giant brain in the sky, nor is He a nameless force. He is Spirit, and He has revealed Himself as having an intellect, a will, and emotions that work together, and so it is with us! Emotions cannot rule, but neither can intellect rule alone. Both must be set in order, along with our will, and ruled by the Holy Spirit as He leads us into all truth. As we enter into a relationship with God the Father through faith in Jesus, a process of restoration and renewal begins that should naturally include all of these aspects of our being. But the reality is that we often find ourselves stuck and in need of emotional healing and freedom that just doesn't seem to come. But if we're doing our best to grow spiritually and to follow Jesus, it should all work itself out, right? So, what's the problem?

I firmly believe that at the cross, Jesus provided fully for our healing and restoration. All the grace necessary has been freely given. There is a vital connection that must be made, however, between the grace that God has provided in the cross of Christ, and those deep places of need that exist in each of us. There is a Bridge, so to speak, over which grace travels, and that bridge is **forgiveness**. This forgiveness is something we receive from God, and that we extend to others precisely *because* we have received it. This is how grace—that provision of God that comes to the point of our need—flows into our lives and into the world in which we live. *This is where I find so many people become stuck.* Often it's not that we are unwilling to forgive or that we have been insincere in our attempts. The problem is often that we haven't truly understood what forgiveness is and how to truly, deeply receive and give it.

Understanding Forgiveness and Emotional Healing

So much has already been written on the subject of forgiveness—precisely because it is such a critical component to mental and emotional health, as well as being central to the gospel—that I almost feel foolish in my attempt to add anything to the discussion...except that in my experience of pastoral counseling, this is where so many people continue to struggle, despite all the teaching and emphasis on forgiveness. I'm convinced that the problem, at least in part, is that our practice of forgiveness has not gone deep enough. We've approached it as a divine command, an obligation for "good" Christians to fulfill, so we have to keep on striving to do it, while we try mightily to beat back the unpleasant emotions, bitterness, and painful memories that threaten to derail our attempts. This type of performance-driven, rule-based, act-of-the-will "forgiveness" falls wide of the mark and completely misses the healing work that our Father God wants to do in us. We need to approach this work of forgiveness in the context of relationship with a good Father who loves us and wants to make us whole.

> Praise be to the God and Father of our Lord Jesus Christ, the Father of compassion and the God of all comfort, who comforts us in all our troubles, so that we can comfort those in any trouble with the comfort we ourselves receive from God (2 Corinthians 1:3–4).

Do you see how God is described here? He is the "Father of compassion" and "the God of all comfort." Comfort is one of those intangible, but nonetheless powerful things, an essential element that is often in short supply in our world. It is especially in short supply in poorly functioning families where adults may not have the capacity, understanding, time, or patience to offer comfort to a sad or suffering child. What is comfort, exactly? To comfort someone is "to offer encouragement and hope, to ease grief or trouble," according to the dictionary. It doesn't seem very practical, but it is powerful. Comfort is that assurance that you are not alone in your sadness, loss, or pain. It's the assurance that you matter, that what you are feeling is real and valid, and that someone else cares that you are suffering. It's the assurance that it's going to be okay. When a child, for example, loses a favorite toy, or falls and scrapes a knee, or perhaps experiences rejection or failure, holding that child while he or she cries, saying, "I know it hurts so bad, but you're going to be okay," is a powerful, necessary thing. It's not "practical," in that comfort doesn't fix the problem or make the pain go away, but it does say, "You matter, your feelings matter, you are loved, and you are important." **Comfort provides an outlet for the emotional pain to be shared, expressed, and ultimately released, instead of stuffed inside and denied.** So many of us didn't know what to do with our griefs and pains as children—or maybe even into our adult lives—so we simply stuffed them down inside and put a lid on them. The problem with that is that we still carry those griefs, and they make life unbearably heavy at times. So, what does this have to do with forgiveness?

Many of us struggle with feelings of worthlessness—not the extreme "I'm a useless worm and I shouldn't even be taking up space on the planet" kind of worthlessness, but that sense that we don't matter very much, and that we certainly don't want to be needy and inconvenience anyone. Most everyone else is more important and deserving... Then we start dealing with God and the Bible, and one of the first major concepts we hear about is forgiveness: Not only have I received it (which is great!), but now I suddenly have to forgive everyone else for whatever they've done to me, no matter what it was, no questions asked. It can feel like déjà vu all over again: My feelings and needs don't matter; what happened to me doesn't matter; I don't matter. God just wants me to forgive everyone and get over it. Although most people won't verbalize it, you could get the impression that God really doesn't care about your suffering, your loss, or the damage others have done to you. He just wants you to "be good"—to stop crying and to not make a fuss. Can't you see that He has enough to worry about without you crying and making things difficult?

So, we say the words "I forgive," and we pronounce a general amnesty, often without really looking at what it is that needs to be forgiven ("Lord, I forgive everyone for everything they've ever done to me, now please take away all these negative feelings. Amen!"). But nothing ever changes.

The truth is that the God who is revealed through Scripture and in Jesus actually cares deeply about our griefs and losses, about the things that have impacted our lives. He has not ignored anything! His intention is to comfort and heal us, and to release us so that we are set free from those heavy bonds that often keep us tied to the past. Often this healing work begins as a decision on our part to forgive, but the act of forgiveness is more of a **process** than a single act.

The biblical word *forgive* means "to release, to remit, to let go, to cancel a debt." It is letting go of the right to hurt those who have hurt me; it is letting go of the demand for payment. Payment for what? Payment for all of the damages and losses that someone else's wrong actions or choices have cost me. In order to forgive honestly and deeply, I need to reckon with what has happened and understand how it has affected me. I need to tally up the cost and then bring it all to the only One who can truly heal and restore, the One who has fully paid the price for every wrong that has ever been committed on the face of the earth—whether you were the victim or the perpetrator.

Isaiah 53:4–5 says it like this:

> Surely he took up our pain and bore our suffering, yet
> we considered him punished by God, stricken by him,
> and afflicted. But he was pierced for our transgressions,
> he was crushed for our iniquities; the punishment that
> brought us peace was on him, and by his wounds we
> are healed.

We human beings are famous for causing damage that we have no ability to fix, but there is a Healer. It is when we stop demanding payment from those who can't really fix it, when we cancel the debt, when we stop trying to get out of people something that only God can do for us, that's when healing comes! Now, to make this practical and doable, here is a simple process that I have found helpful to guide those who are suffering under the weight of the past, and to help them toward emotional freedom and peace:

- Face it—the damage/loss.
- Feel it—the grief, fear, and hurt—and pour it out to the God of all comfort.
- Forgive it—cancel the debt, release the one who has wronged you, and let go of the anger.

Let's talk about these steps in a little more detail. The very thought of dredging up all that junk from the past or even taking a good look at it, stops some people before they begin. "Why do I need to go back and remember all that stuff? Aren't we supposed to forget what is behind and press on?" The fact is, if it really was all in the past, we wouldn't be having such a hard time moving forward. More often than not, what happened back there is still impacting how we function today, and we need to get free. The goal here is to deal with the past, not dwell in it.

1) Face It

If I'm going to forgive, I need to know exactly what it is I am forgiving. What happened, how did it affect me, and what did it cost me? I call this a **damage assessment**. If another driver crashes into your car in the supermarket parking lot, you will get their insurance information so that you can get your vehicle repaired. Before the repair can happen, though, the insurance adjuster is going to come have a close look at your car to see exactly what has been damaged and to calculate how much it will cost to fix it all. The list will be detailed. The adjuster will take photos. What's the point? Is all this focus on the damage so that you can take the photos home, frame them, look at them every day, and cry about it? Of course not! The ultimate goal is to address the damage and repair it, so that you can get on with your life.

So do this: Get a sheet of paper and write at the top the person's name whom you need to forgive. Make three columns. Label the first one "Damages." These are the things that were actively done against you that caused harm (physical or verbal abuse, violence, betrayal, etc.). Be specific. Label the second column "Losses" (what you lost as a result of the wrong done against you: security, confidence, a friendship, trust, a life opportunity, etc.). Also in this column would be losses experienced as a result of abandonment, neglect by a parent, etc. Label the third column as "Impact." Here you will identify the way these damages or losses are still affecting your life today, in things such as behavior, life circumstances, decision-making, relationships, and so on. The purpose here is not to wallow in misery—and it is definitely not to blame others and make excuses—but to clearly identify what needs to be forgiven, and to understand how these issues have continued to impact your life. With this understanding, you can begin to take responsibility for making positive changes and no longer be controlled by the past.

2) Feel It

This is where you bring all the pain, the anger, the sense of loss, and the reality of loss into the presence of God, the Father of mercies and the God of all comfort. Bring your list with you and use it to help you pour out your heart to the Father. Confess all these things to Him—what happened, what it did to you, and the anger, fear, or grief you've carried around. Of course, He already knows all the details, but the Scriptures invite us to "pour our hearts before Him" (Psalm 62:8) and to cast all our cares on Him, because *He* cares (1 Peter 5:7). In this step you are emptying your heart of all the junk that has been stuffed down there, maybe for years, and you're making room to receive the comfort of God.

I realize that this may seem like a lot of "navel-gazing" and rolling around in self-pity, but it is not. This is taking responsibility for what is going on inside of you and dealing with it instead of just living with it. It is taking a deliberate step to empty yourself of all the pain, grief, and often, the anger or resentment you've been carrying around—because it is exhausting to keep a lid on it all the time—and through humble confession to turn from all the unhealthy ways you've tried to manage that pain, and receive the Father's healing grace. I have often found that for those who have difficulty experiencing the presence of God or "feeling" His nearness, this breaks the barrier. Now there is room to receive His comfort, since all the negative and threatening emotions that were filling that space have been let go. You become present to God just as you are in your neediness, and you realize that He has been present all along, loving you just as you are and waiting to heal you.

Sometimes this can be done just between you and the Lord, but I've found that if there are multiple issues (and multiple people to forgive), such as often happens in poorly functioning families where there have been years of dysfunction, and now as an adult you are dragging around a mountain of hurt, it's helpful to have a counselor, or a trusted and mature Christian friend, with you as you pray through your list. They can help you sort through the issues, identify what you're feeling, and help you to stay on track. They can pray for you to receive the grace you need. If the list is long, it may be too overwhelming or just not practical to deal with it all at once. A little at a time is okay, if that's what it takes.

3) Forgive It

Once we have identified the damage and received the comfort of God, which tells us how much we really do matter to Him, and once we have begun to empty out the pain or bitterness, forgiving becomes much more doable. We understand that the person who wounded us cannot heal us, that they can't effectively pay the debt, and so we are ready to cancel the debt and release them. Then we turn to God to fill in the holes and heal the damage.

It's wonderful if those who wronged us can acknowledge what they did and ask our forgiveness—if they can somehow make amends. But even when that happens, it is still God who must heal the damage to the soul and bring restoration. The sad reality is that sometimes we will never get that admission of guilt, and we won't hear those words, "Forgive me." We will never be able to regain the thing that was lost. How often have I observed adult children still striving for the parental approval they never got when they were small, still demanding payment. Still demanding that someone admit how it really was instead of sugarcoating a broken past. It is a useless quest! It's time to let go, release those who "owe" us, and receive the Father's provision of grace in Jesus.

Maybe you are still hanging on to that dream, that plan you had for your life, the way it was supposed to be—and that now never will be. We can hang on to the disappointment of failed expectations, and the disappointment becomes our excuse to remain stuck. Part of forgiveness is letting go of those things, too, releasing it all to the Father and choosing to trust that He is for us, and that He is perfectly able to work all things together for our good and His glory, despite what has happened. He is the good Father and we can trust Him. As we learn to walk the path of forgiveness, to practice it, to receive it, and to give it, we are well on the way to emotional health and freedom, moving forward on our journey to the Father.

A Final Word ...

> Jesus answered, "I am the way and the truth and the
> life. No one comes to the Father except through me"
> (John 14:6).

We are pilgrims in this world, on a lifelong journey, and the destination is the Father. The way that Jesus opened for us, the truth He has revealed, the life He gives—**this** is how we are going to get there. With each phase of our pilgrimage, we learn more of who the Father is and how He works, how strong is His love, how wise are His ways, how firm is His grip on our lives. So, be encouraged! I wish I could wrap my arms around every one of you reading these words and tell you that *yes, you are going to make it!* But since I can't do that, I'll leave you with these words instead:

> **See what great love the Father has lavished on us,**
> **that we should be called children of God! And that**
> **is what we are! The reason the world does not know**
> **us is that it did not know him. Dear friends, now we**
> **are children of God, and what we will be has not yet**
> **been made known. But we know that when Christ**
> **appears, we shall be like him, for we shall see him as**
> **he is** (1 John 3:1–3).

With all my heart, I'm counting on it. We'll see Him as He really is, and we'll see each other, all glorious and free and fully ourselves—children of the good Father for all eternity.